I CAN'T WAIT

I CAN'T WAIT
How to Sustain Passion in an Organization

Copyright © 2024 Michael Beard

ISBN (paperback): 978-1-956220-94-0
ISBN (hardback): 978-1-956220-98-8

This publication is designed to provide accurate and authoritative information regarding the subject matter contained within. It should be understood that the author and publisher are not engaged in rendering legal, accounting, or other financial services through this medium. The author and publisher shall not be liable for your misuse of this material and shall have neither liability nor responsibility to anyone with respect to any loss or damage caused, or alleged to be caused, directly or indirectly by the information contained in this book. The author and/or publisher do not guarantee that anyone following these strategies, suggestions, tips, ideas, or techniques will become successful. If legal advice or other expert assistance is required, the services of a competent professional should be sought.
All rights reserved. No portion of this book may be reproduced mechanically, electronically, or by any other means, including photocopying, without the written permission of the author. It is illegal to copy the book, post it to a website, or distribute it by any other means without permission from the author.

Expert Press
2 Shepard Hills Court
Little Rock, AR 72223
www.ExpertPress.net

Editing by Emmett O'Neill
Editorial contributions by Georgina Chong-You
Copyediting by Hannah Skaggs
Proofreading by Heather Dubnick
Text design and composition by Emily Fritz
Cover design by Casey Fritz

I CAN'T WAIT

HOW TO SUSTAIN PASSION IN AN ORGANIZATION

MICHAEL BEARD

I dedicate this book to my beautiful supportive wife, Dawn; my children, Deylynd and Terrell; and my parents, Martha, Terrell, Lesia, Willie, Denise, and Jimmy.

CONTENTS

FOREWORD	i
INTRODUCTION	**1**
Every Garden Starts with a Single Seed	3
The Core Values of Leadership	5
Rekindling the Spark: The Power of Excitement in Leadership	9
Ja'siah's Story: A Testament to Anticipation and Faith	10
Anticipation: A Recipe for Passion, Productivity, and Persistence	12
What This Book Will Provide	14
1 The Gifts You Give	**17**
Opportunity (and Amazon) Knocks at the Door	19
Unwrapping the Future	21
Inspiring Passion and Keeping Your Vision Fresh	27
Mastering the Exchange: The Art of Receiving Gifts	29
2 The Gifts You Receive	**31**
Four Hats	33
Anticipation: The Passion Pill	35
The Importance of a Leader's Response to Contributions	36
Embracing Vulnerability in Leadership	40
The Gift Exchange Cycle	42
Poorly Wrapped Gifts: The Role of Employees in Gift-Giving	45
By Receiving Gifts Properly, You Increase Your Bounty	47
3 The Atmosphere You Create	**49**
Group Psychology, Team Dynamics, and Optimized Workspaces	51
The Ideal Work Environment	54
How Do I Create This Kind of Environment?	57
The Three Cs: Core Values, Culture, and Community	60

The Atmosphere You Create Is Essential	62
4 Roadblocks	**65**
Unearthing the Roots of a Roadblock	66
Turning Roadblocks into Gateways: Eight Practical Tips	77
Bridging the Gap: Roadblocks and Leadership Barriers	79
5 Barriers to Leadership	**81**
Understanding the Importance of Overcoming Barriers	82
Critical Questions for Self-Evaluation	83
Identifying Bias and Overcoming Personal Obstacles	85
Five Common Barriers and Their Solutions	88
The Greatest Barrier May Be Difficult to Face	93
Overcoming Barriers to Build Bridges	95
6 The Bridge and the Apology	**97**
The Apology	99
Building on the Apology and Establishing a New Baseline for Success	102
The Importance and Impact of Tough Conversations	103
Bridge-Building to Win Sustainably	105
Using Your Bridges: The Role of Goal-Setting	107
What's on the Other Side?	109
CONCLUSION	**111**
Chapter 1: The Gifts You Give	111
Chapter 2: The Gifts You Receive	114
Chapter 3: The Atmosphere You Create	115
Chapter 4: Roadblocks	118
Chapter 5: Barriers to Leadership	120
Chapter 6: The Bridge and the Apology	122
Bring Your Vision to Fruition	124
Contact Information	126
ABOUT THE AUTHOR	**129**

FOREWORD

As I sit down to write this foreword for *I Can't Wait*, a book authored by my dear friend, Michael Beard, I am filled with a sense of pride and admiration that spans over two decades of friendship and professional camaraderie. Michael, who I have had the privilege of knowing since our early days as budding professionals, has blossomed into a leadership guru possessing the remarkable ability to transform anyone into an exceptional leader. His journey, marked by relentless passion, innovative thinking, research, and a deep commitment to transforming mindsets, is not just inspiring but a testament to the power of dedication and vision in shaping minds and the future of organizations.

Dynamic, passionate, and profoundly empathetic, Michael Beard stands out as a shining example of transformative leadership. Michael does not merely teach leadership skills; he embodies them.

Michael has consistently pushed the boundaries of traditional leadership techniques. He has shown an unwavering dedication to innovation, always seeking out new ways to engage, inspire, and motivate leaders. His work is a powerful reminder that leadership is not just about transferring knowledge; it is about transforming lives.

I Can't Wait captures the essence of excitement and promise so compelling that you won't want to put it down. As you begin this book, prepare to embark on a journey with an author who is not only a dynamic force but also a breath of fresh air for all those looking to be better leaders.

Michael's approach to leadership is nothing short of revolutionary. His innovative techniques and deep understanding of organizational and staff developmental needs have made a profound impact on the efficiency and growth of businesses worldwide. His work is not just necessary; it is a game-changer, offering new perspectives and methods that are reshaping our approach to leadership.

Throughout *I Can't Wait*, Michael's talent and passion for leadership development immediately become evident. This book is more than just a collection of ideas; it is a manifesto for change. How we interact with others, and a call to action for all who believe in the transformative power of gift-giving.

Michael's involvement in leadership development has been pivotal. At a time of staff shortages, burnout, and high stress levels, Michael has stepped in and rejuvenated numerous organizations with fresh ideas and innovative strategies, proving to be exactly what is needed to propel businesses forward. His work is not just about imparting knowledge; it is about awakening possibilities, inspiring minds, and fostering an environment where everyone is seen, heard, and valued.

As you turn these pages, get ready to lose yourself in a journey of discovery, learning, and inspiration. No matter what industry you are in, this book will guide you in changing culture and transforming your organization into a more innovative, efficient, and cohesive entity. The journey ahead is not just about learning how to lead; it is about learning how to lead with kindness, vision, and an unwavering commitment. A true testament to the impact one individual can have in shaping the future of leadership development. Michael Beard is not just a contributor to the field of leadership; he is a trailblazer, paving the way for a brighter, more innovative future for all leaders.

—Dr. Robert Welch, Director of Tri-County Youth and Development Council

INTRODUCTION

Source: Elevated Leadership

In my years of navigating the intricate facets of leadership, I've come to recognize the profound impact that human connections and vision can hold. They're topics that we often overlook, yet they are the very cornerstone of transformative influence. As we begin this book, I want to start with a story that exemplifies the importance of these subjects and illustrates the very essence of what it means to be a visionary and empathetic leader. That story is the Feeding of the Five Thousand, a miracle of such distinct significance that it found a place in all four gospels in the New Testament.

I want you to cast your mind back thousands of years to a remote area near the Sea of Galilee. Our story begins with Jesus Christ amid a vast expanse of weary followers. The expressions on their faces are clear: these people are desperate, hungry, and far from the solace of their homes. Jesus's disciples, wary of the overwhelming numbers, advise caution; they suggest it would be best to disperse the crowd or find safety. Yet, in this moment of uncertainty, Jesus does not flee. He chooses to see the situation not as a problem but as an opportunity to demonstrate the power of vision and faith.

With only two fish and five loaves of bread, a meager offering for such a multitude, Jesus showcases two fundamental leadership principles: empathy and resourcefulness in the face of scarcity. He takes what little they have, offers gratitude, and shares it among the hungry masses. The result? Not only are all fed, but there are leftovers to spare—an abundance created from what initially seemed insufficient.

This miracle is not just about feeding the hungry; it's a valuable lesson for all who seek to lead. Jesus shows compassion and understanding of his followers' needs, just as a leader must attune to the needs of their team. He demonstrates innovation and resourcefulness, turning a seemingly impossible situation into a triumph. Most importantly, he stays true to his vision and values while involving his disciples in the process, empowering them to be part of the solution.

Jesus and other great leaders like him show us that the outcomes of our endeavors directly connect to the relationships we nurture along the way. This approach isn't just about fostering a pleasant work environment; it's about creating a world where people feel genuinely valued and understood. Doing so begins by recognizing the problems facing modern organizations and understanding that solutions lie not in the destination but in how we get there.

EVERY GARDEN STARTS WITH A SINGLE SEED

My voyage into transformative leadership didn't begin in a boardroom or at a leadership seminar; it started with a friendly conversation with a fraternity brother. He was struggling in his new position as executive director of a large business in Iowa; the company was faltering quickly, and he was worried it might fail. So he turned to me for help, and a short time later, my advice ended up helping him turn the business around. He was incredibly grateful—so grateful, in fact, that he spread the word quickly to everyone he knew.

For the next two weeks, it felt like giving leadership advice had become a full-time job for me. During this time I realized that a majority of the complaints my friends and family shared were rooted in the same glaring problem: selfish leadership. Their bosses, their supervisors, their company owners—many lacked a clear sense of empathy or interest in their people. All they cared about were results.

This realization created the book you hold in your hands now. Over the years, as I've advised and mentored leaders in various fields, I've realized this wasn't an isolated trend. In industries and organizations around the world, there is a severe lack of genuine people-focused leadership. Instead, many managers and executives are trapped in an endless loop of using and losing staff, wringing people for every last drop of work while continually asking, "Why do we have so much turnover?" These leaders never realize the massive potential they could reach by developing their existing team's talents, recognizing individual achievement, and cultivating passion instead of draining it away. The ripples of a people-centric approach are far-reaching, affecting not just our workplaces but our homes, our well-being, and our very perceptions of what it means to lead and be led.

In my own journey, I've seen firsthand the transformative power of putting people first. The idea is simple yet profound: when we focus on the person, positive outcomes inevitably follow. This book is a reflection of that philosophy, a distillation of my years of experience as a business, religious, and motivational leader and a testament to my belief that the most prosperous path doesn't just follow the numbers—it's one you and your employees find together when you share your vision, inspire passion, and stoke the burning fires that motivate success and innovation. To do this, I rely on three core values of leadership.

THE CORE VALUES OF LEADERSHIP

In every aspect of my life, from delivering sermons and motivational talks to consulting with business leaders and providing for my family, I consistently anchor my actions in three fundamental principles:

- Being people-centered
- Being growth-minded
- Being driven to empower

Whether I'm in a boardroom, at the pulpit, or at the dinner table, these values are the lenses through which I view the world around me. They shape not just how I lead, but how I connect, grow, and inspire everyone I interact with. And they can do the same for you.

Core Value 1: Being People-Centered

*We don't use people to get the job done;
we use the job to get people done.*

Staying people-centered means prioritizing the well-being and aspirations of your team members and seeing them as whole individuals beyond their professional roles. In practice, this involves three intentional practices:

- Actively listening to team members
- Genuinely addressing their concerns
- Creating an inclusive environment where everyone feels valued

I can tell you from experience, the impact of such an approach is profound. In a short time, you will foster a workplace culture of loyalty and belonging, enhance team cohesion, and cause morale to skyrocket. By truly understanding and valuing each team member, you can build a more positive work environment while increasing satisfaction and engagement.

Core Value 2: Being Growth-Minded

We commit to continuous improvement and growth at every level.

Adopting a growth mindset is central to my leadership ideology. It's all about encouraging continuous learning and embracing challenges as opportunities for development. Implementing this involves three more intentional practices:

- Providing professional development opportunities
- Promoting creative problem-solving
- Recognizing the progress and effort of your team

The results of fostering a growth mindset within your team are invaluable. You'll see more innovation, adaptability, and resilience, keeping both individuals and the organization agile and forward-looking as your vision takes shape.

Core Value 3: Being Driven to Empower

We encourage empowerment, not control.

Being driven to empower is about equipping your team with the resources, confidence, and autonomy they need to succeed. In practice, you'll focus on these efforts:

- Delegating meaningful responsibilities
- Trusting team members with the freedom to take initiative
- Supporting them in their professional growth

The effect of this empowerment is a higher level of engagement and productivity. It cultivates leadership qualities within the team, fostering a sense of ownership and accountability for their work. When people feel empowered, they are creative, proactive, and committed to the organization's collective success.

These principles not only fuel the engines of my personal success but also allow me to propel individuals within my organizations to heights they never thought imaginable. But simply knowing these values isn't enough. There needs to be a genuine excitement behind their implementation, an excitement many people lose as time goes on.

REKINDLING THE SPARK: The Power of Excitement in Leadership

This book is an invitation—to business owners, to leaders old and new, to anyone who finds themselves in a position of influence—to embark on a journey of rediscovery. Think back to when you first started in your profession. Remember that sense of being on the edge of something great? There's a drive in those early days that compels us forward into priceless moments of exploration and cutting-edge experimentation. That spark is a combination of anticipation, eagerness, and a touch of nervous energy. It creates a powerful force that drives our creativity, pushes our boundaries, and fuels our desire to explore the unknown.

Everyone can remember a time when their mind was ripe with possibilities, teeming with ideas waiting to be unleashed. Your capacity for innovation was at its peak; every challenge seemed surmountable, and you could achieve anything. I intend to help you rekindle that spark we all felt at the start of our careers and to remind you of why you chose your path in the first place. Once you find your spark, you can use it to ignite the fires of progress and passion within each and every member of your organization. One of the best ways to do this is with a secret ingredient many fail to recognize: anticipation.

JA'SIAH'S STORY: A Testament to Anticipation and Faith

Before delving into the heart of anticipation's role in leadership and personal growth, it's crucial to acknowledge a fundamental truth: Anticipation is a choice, and its mantle rests not only on the shoulders of leaders but also on every team member. The presentation of anticipation as a worthwhile weight to be worn by the leader does not exempt team members from their part in this dynamic. Every individual, regardless of their position, has the agency to choose anticipation as their lens for viewing challenges and opportunities. This shared commitment to a forward-looking perspective is what transforms potential into progress.

To illustrate the power of anticipation, I want to share a story about my eleven-year-old cousin, Ja'siah. Ja'siah loved school, and he loved church. Tragically, his life was cut short in an instant on a November afternoon, when a distracted driver, preoccupied with his phone, failed to see Ja'siah as he crossed the street to board his school bus. This loss sent ripples of despair through our family. We were no strangers to tragedy–I had lost another cousin, four-year-old Toya, in the same way, some years before. But that didn't make this loss any less traumatic.

I rushed to the hospital immediately after hearing of Ja'siah's car accident. Once I got there, my extended family was distraught, crying, mourning the loss of someone who was gone far too young. After comforting them, my first thought was "How do I tell my son?" Terrell had a practice that evening, and as I picked him up, I braced myself for a difficult conversation.

"Terrell, I've got some bad news. Your cousin Ja'siah has passed away."
"Dad, he died? He died?"
"Yes son, he died."
"So Ja'siah's with Jesus?"
"Yeah, he's with Jesus."
"So, Ja'siah's in heaven?"
"Yeah, I definitely think Ja'siah is in heaven."

My son laid back in his seat and looked out at the window, staring up into the clouds for a moment. Then he sat up, slapped his hand in his fist, and exclaimed "Dad, so you are trying to tell me that

Ja'siah is with Jesus *right now*?" I nodded my head, and he smiled. "I can't wait to see Jesus!"

In the midst of this profound sorrow, my son Terrell's response was both surprising and enlightening. Rather than dwelling on the loss, he embraced a sense of joy, uplifted by the anticipation of something greater waiting ahead. It wasn't as though the facts of the situation had changed, but rather how Terrell had chosen to view them. His approach serves as a powerful lesson for leaders: In the face of adversity, the perspective we choose can either anchor us in despair or buoy us with hope. Instead of being weighed down by what we've lost, we have to harness the power of anticipation and look toward the possibilities our journey still holds for us.

ANTICIPATION: A Recipe for Passion, Productivity, and Persistence

In my opinion, anticipation is one of the least utilized tools in leadership. At its core, anticipation in leadership is about creating a sense of passion and exhilaration for the future. You'll need to paint a vivid picture of what lies ahead, not just for the organization but for everyone within it. This sense of anticipation keeps teams motivated, engaged, and focused on goals.

While I've seen the power of anticipation firsthand, this isn't just based on personal observations; scientific evidence supports it. A 2017 study, *Well-Being and Anticipation for Future Positive Events*,[1] shows that when we anticipate positive events, there's a significant activation in the medial prefrontal cortex, an area of the brain linked to well-being. This activation is not just a fleeting reaction; it's a neural indication that looking forward to positive events can genuinely enhance our sense of well-being and, by extension, our productivity. Now, imagine harnessing this kind of anticipation in our workplaces. If we, as leaders, can create an environment where our team members eagerly anticipate positive outcomes, think of the productivity leap we could achieve.

Using anticipation isn't a mere motivation trick; I'm talking about tapping into a fundamental aspect of human psychology. To do this, CEOs, managers, and supervisors need to be willing to do more than routine management. You will need a robust and living vision with the agile ability to adapt to your unique challenges. Your vision and the anticipation you build around it will shape your work environment into an organic being, one that will be capable of sustaining

---

[1] Yangmei Luo, Xuhai Chen, Senqing Qi, Xuqun You, and Xiting Huang, "Well-Being and Anticipation for Future Positive Events: Evidences from an fMRI Study," *Frontiers in Psychology* 8 (2018): 2199, https://doi.org/10.3389/fpsyg.2017.02199.

those within it. By doing this, you can breathe new life into your organization, treating those you lead not as cogs in a machine but as inhabitants of a community striving for the betterment of all.

WHAT THIS BOOK WILL PROVIDE

So, what can you expect from these pages? Well, if you came looking for another leadership manual filled with fluff and abstract theories, you'll be disappointed. This is a practical guide infused with real-life examples, personal experiences, and actionable strategies. It's a tool to help new and seasoned business owners identify, create, and sustain passion within their organization. In the following chapters, I will reveal the incredible power of human-centric leadership and show you the blueprint for building a culture in which every member feels valued, understood, and motivated.

What I've written here is not just a collection of empty platitudes. It's a vital resource for those who want to transform from ineffective managers into inspirational, empowering, and uplifting leaders. Embracing these concepts will require a commitment to change—not just in your professional life but also in your personal outlook. It's about adopting a mindset in which your people are as important, if not more, than your bottom line.

In the following pages, we will explore the art of leading with passion, the science of fostering anticipation, and the magic of transforming workplaces into spaces of growth, innovation, and heartfelt connection. I'll illustrate the importance of the gifts you give, and the gifts you receive, as a leader. Using my core values, I'll show you how to build unshakeable bridges between the levels of your organization, ones that will allow you to overcome any roadblocks or barriers you may face along the way.

As we traverse this path together, I ask only one thing: come along with an open mind and a willing heart. Trust me, trust the process, and I promise you'll discover not only the joy of leading but the joy of changing lives.

If you're anything like me, there's only one response when someone asks you to embark on a mission of this magnitude: I can't wait.

THE GIFTS YOU GIVE

Remember this: Whoever sows sparingly will also reap sparingly, and whoever sows generously will also reap generously. Each of you should give what you have decided in your heart to give, not reluctantly or under compulsion, for God loves a cheerful giver.

2 Corinthians 9:6-8

Source: Elevated Leadership

In our consumer-driven world, the term *gift* often conjures up images of glossy packages, branded logos, and hefty price tags. This mindset has fostered a stigma, intertwining the very idea of giving with material possessions and monetary value but ignoring the deeper values that make the act of giving significant and meaningful. The power of a gift isn't in what someone spends; it's in the anticipation it creates and how it can change the life of the receiver. As a leader, the greatest gift you can give your team is one that costs nothing to share but can be worth millions, or even billions, if implemented correctly. It also has the power to radically shape an organization's future and benefit everyone who takes part. That gift is your vision.

Some leaders believe their vision was a gift bestowed specifically on them, a gift they can keep to themselves if they so choose. The reality is your vision exists so that you can provide it to others. An unshared vision is unlikely to come to fruition, which is why it's so important to avoid the selfish impulse to hoard it or hide it away. Think of what would have happened if a skilled painter like Van Gogh had hidden his God-given gift instead of displaying it on a canvas for all to see. What if a talented singer like Whitney Houston had chosen to simply sing in the shower instead of sharing her artistic vision with the world? When you have the gift of a great vision, it's your responsibility to share and act on it.

As leaders, satisfying this responsibility begins with determining what makes a gift so valuable. By doing this, we can understand how to wrap our vision, build anticipation, and unveil it to others in a way that best shows the depth of our passion and commitment. To show you what I mean, I want to start with a personal story that demonstrates why the anticipation and opening of a gift can be just as important as what's inside.

OPPORTUNITY (AND AMAZON) KNOCKS AT THE DOOR

Like many of you, my wife Dawn loves to shop on Amazon. Every day there are one or two (and sometimes ten) boxes sitting on the front step when I get home from work. Now, she isn't ordering anything crazy; my wife is a very frugal person. But still, the boxes pile up, and because we share an Amazon account, they have my name on them. This point will be important later on—trust me.

So I get home one day and see a single Amazon package with my name on it sitting at the front door. *I might have ordered something*, I thought, but couldn't remember what, so I took the box inside. For some reason, not knowing what that box held made opening it up exciting; even though I knew it was probably just office supplies or something I needed for work, not knowing what was in there built up a profound feeling of anticipation. As my fingers pulled back the tape and I tore open the top of the box, I looked in to see that it was nothing more than a plain old box of Q-tips.

Oh, I guess I didn't order anything, I thought. *Hmm.* Thinking nothing of it, I set the box aside and used the rest of my day to spend quality time with my son.

When Dawn arrived home, I heard her yell up to the balcony. "Who opened my box?" She squinted at me, holding the opened box up like evidence in a courtroom.

"Oh, I did."
"Why did you open it?"
"Well, the box had my name on it, it had my address, and it was on my Amazon account. So, I opened it."
"But did you order anything?"
"No, I didn't."

My wife's eyes narrowed even further, and she pointed at me with purpose. "Don't open my box!"

So, how did I respond? How did I handle that situation? Some of you might think I should have told her I wouldn't be spoken to that way. But I didn't do that, for two reasons: One, because I'm not out of my mind. And two, because I realized part of what made her angry.

See, all that box contained was Q-tips. Are Q-tips useful? Absolutely, but they were certainly not something she particularly cared about. No, she was mad because she didn't get to open the box herself. That anticipation, that dopamine rush, the blood vessels opening up and flooding with endorphins—I had taken away an opportunity, a chance to participate in the process of discovery.

Now, how does this apply to leadership? Well, think of the chemical processes that go into opening a gift, even one that contains something as utilitarian or mundane as Q-tips. As leaders, we must create that same anticipation and passion within our organization. When you present your vision to your team, it isn't just a declaration of objectives or goals. It's an unveiling of opportunities, an invitation to a shared journey.

UNWRAPPING THE FUTURE

This revelation is especially pivotal in the early days of any leadership role. During this period, many of us experience what I call our "State of the Union" moment. It's that pivotal juncture when you have the responsibility to reflect on an organization's past, assess its present, and paint a vivid picture of its future. This moment often takes the form of a presentation given either to a small coalition of executives and managers or to your organization as a whole. To better understand this, we can envision the process as the three components of a gift.

The Box: Reflection and Legacy

The beginning of any new leadership journey can be a bit dicey, as the responsibility of addressing your organization's history (both good and bad) falls on your shoulders. In these moments, it's often tempting to critique the decisions of past leaders. For those who have been in a particular organization for a while and risen through the ranks, there were probably moments when you criticized previous leaders for the job they were doing, telling others how things would be different if you were in charge. Now that the anticipation phase is over and you're in the hot seat, you'll be surprised how quickly those tables can turn.

So, instead of using this time as an opportunity to cast stones, it's better to recognize the achievements of those who came before you. Highlight the actions of key players, applaud the trailblazers, and celebrate important milestones. Acknowledge the fact that the organization wouldn't be around today without your predecessors' hard work and dedication. By choosing to shine a spotlight instead of casting shadows, you start your tenure by showing your faith in your organization's legacy and your respect for its past leadership. This conviction and confidence, along with your honest assessment of the past, functions as the Box: the foundation on which you can build your organization's future.

The Wrapping: A Picture of the Present
This part of the process should be an honest assessment of where the organization is today. You'll dive into the strategies the company has used to achieve its success, which quotas and objectives are being met, and what headway has been made on major projects. You'll also go through your organization's strengths and weaknesses, areas where it has recently made progress, and areas where it can still improve.

When it comes to this last line item, remember the lessons learned from discussing your organization's past and avoid naming names; this part is more about giving a status report on the organization as a whole. If possible, sandwich the more critical aspects of this section (current weaknesses) between more positive components (current strengths.) Overall, this assessment helps to create a baseline perspective of where your organization is while showing why change is necessary and leaving room for future growth. Once established, this perspective serves as The Wrapping: the appearance of your organization at this moment.

The Gift: Your Vision for the Future

Just as a magician leaves the biggest trick for last, the conclusion of your presentation will involve the grand unveiling of your vision for the future. Keep in mind that these plans should be less about you as an individual and more about the organization and those within it. Think about it this way: If you're the captain of a ship and are telling your crew that you've spotted an island, you aren't going to motivate them by talking about filling the captain's quarters with treasure. Instead, your team needs to understand how *they* will benefit and what their role will be in this new journey.

Now, if we remember the story with my wife, Dawn, we can see how people feel if they don't get to participate in the unwrapping of a gift. If you want your team to feel that crucial rush of motivation, anticipation, and adrenaline, you'll need to make them understand how they will actively participate in your vision. For example, let's say that recent cutbacks have left your organization understaffed. Your teams have reported feeling overworked; without the implementation of a viable plan, you can tell that burnout is on the horizon. So, what do you do?

In this scenario, the best course of action is to create a clear solution with a solid timeline. During your initial presentation, you can announce that you intend to fully staff the organization within two years. Now, this solution will create anticipation on its own, but to really seal the deal, you'll need to show your team how they will directly participate and benefit.

One way to do this could be to weave incentives into the structure of your employee restaffing program. For example, you could announce that a number of key staff members will be promoted to training positions and supervisory roles. This announcement creates anticipation on two levels: one, it provides the potential for promotion, which is always a powerful motivator. And two, the internal promotion of existing team members to training positions indicates that these new hires will become valuable far more quickly. In one fell swoop, you've given your team a light at the end of the tunnel to get them through that burnout, which will revitalize their motivation through the coming months as you begin to implement your vision.

Overall, the finale of your presentation should function as a microcosm of your organization's transformation. You will symbolically peel back the Wrapping (what your organization is), open up the Box (what it was), and reveal the Gift (what your organization will be). In a short amount of time, you will have reinforced the foundational elements of what got your organization to where it is today, given a clear perspective on what it looks like now, and established how everyone will prosper in the future. Of course, sharing the gift of your vision isn't just a one-time thing. To be a genuinely effective and selfless leader, you must stoke the fire of passion many times as your vision comes to fruition.

INSPIRING PASSION AND KEEPING YOUR VISION FRESH

One common misconception about having a vision is that it remains static, but this couldn't be further from the truth. For your teams to have a sustained and continuous sense of passion, they need to continue to have that powerful feeling of opening a gift time and time again. If your teams are lacking in passion and lack interest in what they are doing, either you're the wrong leader or they're the wrong followers. If they are the right followers, it's your job to keep the spark of that passion alive. If they aren't, it's also your responsibility as a leader to discern whether they are right for your organization. Doing this will not only keep your vision fresh but keep progress moving. Remember, challenges like these aren't setbacks; they're setups for greater achievements in the future.

To keep your vision fresh, you'll need to ask yourself a few critical questions:

- Are your ideas creative, and do they push the envelope?
- Are you maintaining the same structure your organization had before?
- Are you offering anything new to your team?
- Are you maintaining a high level of effort?
- Are your policies and processes consistently being improved?
- Do you take employee feedback into account?
- How do you show appreciation to team members for their hard work?
- How often do you reflect on your vision's progress?
- How frequently are you engaging with your team to align them with your vision?
- Are you pushing everyone to reach their full potential?

By answering these questions regularly, you can help revitalize and reinforce your vision during key moments in the future. Depending on the nature of your operation, it may be helpful to do this on a monthly or quarterly basis. You can use your answers to check your progress toward short-term and long-term goals or to set new goals if you've noticed some areas aren't meeting the standards of your organization.

MASTERING THE EXCHANGE: The Art of Receiving Gifts

Of course, the gift of your vision is only half of the equation; you also need to think about how you receive the gifts of others. Contrary to what some may believe, the act of receiving gifts is not passive—it's an active engagement that calls for awareness, appreciation, and a keen sense of the value brought forth by those you lead. Flourishing in your role begins with understanding leadership as a two-way street illuminated by the exchange of gifts in both directions. In our next chapter, we'll look at the best way to receive gifts, how your reactions to these gifts can shape future performance, and the precise processes surrounding the Gift Exchange Cycle.

2
THE GIFTS YOU RECEIVE

Source: Elevated Leadership

In leadership, the most extraordinary gifts we receive are often invisible. These gifts are tucked away, hidden in the talents, insights, and energies of those we lead. In many cases, these intangible attributes and contributions offer more value than any physical gift ever could. Embracing and nurturing these gifts is essential, not only for the immediate benefits they bring but for the individual and team growth they can foster. Recognizing the unique qualities of each individual rather than seeing them as mere cogs in the machine is a key aspect of this process.

Think of this concept as tending a garden. In this garden, each team member is a distinct plant with their own unique needs and potential. Some will be like sun-loving flowers, thriving on independence and needing little help, while others will be like shade-seeking ferns, requiring more support and guidance. As a leader, you are the gardener providing the right environment for each plant to bloom without altering their inherent nature. And just as a gardener receives the gift of a harvest from well-tended plants, a leader receives the gift of growth and innovation from well-supported team members.

In this sense, transformational leadership goes beyond traditional management. It's a reciprocal path, one that's not solely about imparting wisdom or directives but also about being open and receptive. It involves valuing and utilizing the unique gifts your team members bring to the table. The success of a visionary leader hinges on understanding and leveraging these varied perspectives and talents. To do this, you must get to know the members of your organization on a personal level.

Let me take you back to a moment with my friend Dr. Robert Welch, to an experience that profoundly reshaped my understanding of these dynamics. It's a tale that demonstrates how truly understanding someone, whether they are a friend or an employee, can make a positive impact on relationships and on the cycle of giving and receiving gifts.

FOUR HATS

To give some background to this story, it's important to know that Robert is an avid collector of hats. Shortly after he received his doctorate, I decided to give him a gift that would both celebrate this milestone and resonate with his passion for headwear. Instead of grabbing one hat at random, I chose a selection of four different ball caps, each uniquely engraved with "Doc," a nod to his recent accomplishment. Each hat was carefully designed with Robert's preferences in mind, not just reflecting his new status as a doctor but serving as a message of deep personal understanding and appreciation for our friendship.

Robert picked me up from the airport, and we drove to his home while talking about one of our biggest shared interests: basketball. The whole time we were talking, I was brimming (no pun intended) with anticipation, excited to share these gifts and celebrate his accomplishment. Once we got to his house, he showed me to his guest room and let me know everything was set up.

As he was leaving, I casually told him, "Oh before you go, I got something for you." As I took the hats out one by one, I could see him get more and more excited; at one point, he literally started to jump up and down. Mind you, Robert is six foot five, but in an instant, he was a kid again.

He finally calmed down for a moment, looked at each of the four hats, and said, "No one knows me like you do."

This moment with Robert, seeing his unbridled joy and genuine appreciation, was more rewarding to me than any gift I could have received. As I watched his excitement, an important realization struck me: the true joy of giving a gift was not in the giving but in witnessing the impact of my gesture. My anticipation of Robert's reaction, the eagerness to see his face light up, was a gift in itself, one more gratifying than any I had ever received. It underscored a vital lesson in leadership: the joy we find in the happiness and growth of those we can lead can be the most rewarding experience of all.

Reflecting on this sense of fulfillment underscores the profound role of anticipation in our experiences, both personally and in our roles as leaders. Just as I found joy in anticipating Robert's reaction, a leader can foster a sense of anticipation and excitement within their team.

ANTICIPATION: The Passion Pill

An often understated aspect of leadership is the role of anticipation in team dynamics, particularly in the context of giving and receiving gifts. Anticipation goes beyond just the expectation of contributions from team members; it encompasses the excitement and potential everyone brings to the table. As a leader, recognizing and nurturing this sense of anticipation can profoundly influence your team's morale and productivity.

I've always considered anticipation as the "passion pill." This metaphorical pill, when administered correctly, acts as a catalyst that ignites positivity and motivation within your team. Imagine a scenario in which a team is working toward a product launch, one they are collectively involved in and genuinely excited about. The anticipation of the launch's success creates a buzz, energizing the team and enhancing their dedication to the project. As a result, they are more inclined to meet deadlines and overcome burnout. Their anticipation functions like a performance-enhancing drug, driving them forward to meet their goal.

In the modern workplace, we frequently overlook the simple yet powerful concept of looking forward to something. You've heard thought leaders emphasize the importance of being "forward-looking," but what does that really mean? In practice, it entails creating an environment where team members have compelling goals and milestones to look forward to. When they do, everyday tasks cease to be mundane; instead, they become stepping stones toward something greater and more exciting.

Understanding the role of anticipation in driving team engagement leads us to another critical facet of leadership: the importance of how we respond to team contributions or how we receive the gifts of those we lead. Our reactions can either amplify or dampen the rhythm of motivation and anticipation within our organization. If we behave correctly, these responses can plant the seeds of enthusiasm and set the tone for subsequent projects.

THE IMPORTANCE OF A LEADER'S RESPONSE TO CONTRIBUTIONS

I learned a vital lesson early in my role as a leader: the most valuable gifts may not always come in the neatest packages. Regardless of how a gift appears, it's crucial to respond constructively to encourage growth and improvement. Let me share a slice of my personal life that captures this principle. It's a story about my wife, Dawn, and her journey into the world of cooking.

When Dawn and I first got married, she made it clear that she was not a cook. Coming from a family where her mother, a dedicated postal worker for thirty years, didn't spend much time in the kitchen, cooking was not something Dawn was familiar with. Initially I accepted this, knowing we could simply pick something up to eat if we needed to. However, I soon realized that we were relying too much on fast food, and I decided to take on the responsibility of cooking for the family.

I cooked various dishes, which the kids absolutely loved, as they weren't used to home-cooked meals. This went on until one evening, I came home to find Dawn cooking.

"I knew you'd be tired," she said. "I wanted to give you a break." This was a pivotal moment. I knew I had to respond in a way that would encourage her despite her lack of experience in the kitchen.

I gathered our boys and instructed them to simply thank their mother for the meal, regardless of how it tasted. And I have to be honest here: That night the rice was crunchy and the meal was far from perfect. Still, the kids and I expressed our heartfelt gratitude.

Later Dawn approached me, acknowledging that her rice wasn't quite like mine, and asked for pointers. I was more than happy to guide her, but what I think was truly impactful was that initial "Thank you." I'm not sure what kind of cook she would be today if I had received her initial efforts poorly.

Fast-forward to the present, and Dawn has become an incredible cook. That simple gratitude ignited her passion for cooking, which has only grown with continued encouragement and guidance. Today our family appreciates her cooking so much that our son, who attends a university two hours away, will drive back home just to enjoy a meal she's prepared.

Better Responses = Better Future Performance
Dawn's story illustrates a fundamental truth in leadership: the way we respond to contributions profoundly influences future performance. Our reactions set the tone for the team's dynamic, creating a cycle of positive reinforcement. By recognizing and valuing each contribution, we fuel anticipation and enthusiasm, encouraging team members to engage more deeply and frequently.

It's crucial to understand that the value of a team member's idea or work lies not only in the final product but in the journey toward it. Recognizing the effort, intent, and thought process behind their actions is key. By appreciating every facet of these contributions, we cultivate an environment where anticipation of future achievements propels continual progress.

To effectively establish a nurturing environment to receive gifts, consider these key practices.

Clear Communication of Vision
Understanding your own vision is certainly important, but it's equally important that every team member grasps it too. Ensure that everyone in your organization can see the bigger picture and understands

how their individual contributions fit in. This clarity helps team members align their efforts with overall objectives, making the integration of their ideas more seamless and impactful.

Openness to Ideas

You need to make it crystal clear that not only are you willing to hear the perspectives of your employees, but you are filled with anticipation at the idea of a fresh take or contribution. Each received gift is an opportunity to demonstrate your openness; as you treat each of these contributions as important and unique, word will spread, encouraging more team members to share their own gifts.

Recognition and Celebration

Just as we anticipate and celebrate milestones in our personal lives, you should do the same in your organization. Create incentive programs, throw a party when a sales goal is met, or take your team out to dinner after a successful quarter. Make sure to recognize all achievements in some way, whether big or small. This practice acknowledges hard work and builds a culture that is always looking forward to future accomplishments.

Overall, anticipating gifts is more than just waiting for something to fall into your lap. It's an active, dynamic process that can drive significant growth and achievement when managed effectively. However, facilitating this process will take something that many leaders aren't comfortable with: vulnerability.

EMBRACING VULNERABILITY IN LEADERSHIP

I want to correct a common misconception right now. Vulnerability isn't about weakness. It's about courage—the courage to be human, acknowledge our limitations, and connect with other individuals on a deeper level. If you're going to create a close connection like I have with Dr. Welch or be able to guide someone like I did with Dawn, you're going to have to be vulnerable.

Part of this vulnerability is admitting it when we don't have all the answers. As leaders, we sometimes believe our role is to be an unshakeable pillar of knowledge and strength. However, true strength comes from acknowledging that the collective wisdom of the team is greater than that of any single individual. If you can't accept this truth, you may miss out on a gift that could lead to greater success for your organization.

One tool that can help you improve your comfort with vulnerability and connect with team members is active listening. This skill goes beyond just hearing words; it involves fully engaging with a team member's perspective. In the hustle of daily operations, it's easy to overlook this aspect, but active listening is crucial for preventing misunderstandings and showing respect for each team member's ideas and concerns. It makes individuals feel valued and heard, laying the groundwork to build anticipation and understand their needs and desires.

By embracing vulnerability, leaders create a space where everyone feels safe to be open and share their gifts, knowing they will be properly received and appreciated. This approach is a cornerstone of the Gift Exchange Cycle, a system that thrives on mutual respect and gratitude.

THE GIFT EXCHANGE CYCLE

At the heart of team interactions and morale lies the Gift Exchange Cycle. This pivotal cycle begins with a simple yet profound realization: every team member has unique gifts to offer. No two team members are exactly alike. Whether it's a creative idea, a specialized skill, a practical solution, or an extra burst of effort when most needed, everyone has a special gift to contribute to this continuous cycle.

The way the cycle operates within a team can significantly impact productivity. A healthy Gift Exchange Cycle fosters an environment of mutual respect, appreciation, and collaboration. It encourages team members to bring their best selves to the table because they know that both they and their contributions will be valued and respected.

On the other hand, a dysfunctional Gift Exchange Cycle (in which contributions are ignored, undervalued, or poorly received) can lead to a decline in morale. Team members may feel undervalued or unappreciated, leading to a decrease in their motivation to contribute actively.

Consequences of Receiving Gifts Poorly
Receiving gifts poorly can have several negative consequences for your team:

- Demotivation: If team members do not feel appreciated for their effort or receive

constant negative critiques, they may lose the motivation to contribute further.
- **Decreased creativity and innovation:** A lack of appreciation can stifle creativity, as team members may hesitate to bring forward innovative ideas for fear that they will be undervalued or dismissed.
- **Erosion of trust:** Poor reception of contributions can erode trust between team members and leaders. Over time, this can lead to a less cohesive team environment.

These negative effects can happen in a number of ways. Say, for example, that a team member brings up an idea in a meeting. For whatever reason—they don't see the value in the idea, don't like how it is packaged, or have a personal problem with that individual—the leader doesn't receive the idea well. In the future, the contributing team member won't be as likely to give their input. Soon this mindset will spread, and the leader will quickly find themselves in a room full of people who have nothing to contribute.

Nurturing a Positive Gift Exchange Cycle

To avoid these consequences, it's vital to nurture a positive cycle. To do this, leaders must be conscious of how they receive and value each contribution. A good reception typically includes the components below:

- **Active listening:** As mentioned above, active listening involves paying attention to what team members are saying and intentionally participating in conversations. This can show your interest and ensure that you give each idea the attention it deserves.
- **Constructive feedback:** By making your feedback constructive, you can make sure that the contributor has a tangible way to reflect and improve for the future. Negative feedback that does nothing but belittle or insult is a surefire way to ensure an employee never shares an idea again.
- **Recognition and appreciation:** Regularly acknowledging and appreciating the efforts and contributions of team members will ensure they are excited to share their gifts, which will spark others to do the same.

Of course, the health of the Gift Exchange Cycle is affected not only by how leaders receive gifts but by how team members present them. The presentation of these gifts–their packaging, if you will–plays a critical role in how they are received and perceived and whether they are properly utilized.

POORLY WRAPPED GIFTS: The Role of Employees in Gift-Giving

Receiving poorly presented ideas is always challenging, but as leaders, we must recognize the value behind these contributions. A "bad package" can take multiple forms. Sometimes it's a result of poor presentation, sometimes it comes from an untrustworthy source, and other times it's simply communicated ineffectively. Seeing through a bad package to the true value of the gift within takes a discerning eye and a deep understanding of one's team—attributes any good leader needs to acquire.

To show you what I mean, let me share a story from my youth. In my neighborhood, we used to have a woman who sold these amazing cakes. She baked all kinds, including chocolate, pound cake, and pineapple upside-down cake, but we always got the red velvet cakes. They were the shiniest, most moist red velvet cakes I'd ever seen, with just the right number of nuts in each layer. These things were amazing, and my grandmother would always send me down to the delivery car to get us both a slice.

One day, a different car than usual pulled up. The cake lady was sick, but my grandmother recognized her mom behind the wheel, so she sent me down. When I got to the window, I looked inside to see that the interior of the car was in horrible shape. The smell was awful, and the cakes, while wrapped and still delicious, were sitting on top of stained seats. She asked me how many slices I needed, to which I quickly responded, "Oh, I'm good," and quickly ran back home.

Even though I thought the cake might still be good, everything around it made the idea of eating it undesirable. As leaders, we often face similar scenarios. A team member might present an idea or a solution that, while potentially valuable, is shrouded by negative elements or poor presentation. It's our job to look beyond the surface, dig up the potential, and give feedback to help our team members improve their ability to deliver their gifts.

As you can see from my cake story, the way a person presents their gift can be just as important as the gift itself. If the cake, despite being delicious, could be rejected due to its presentation, the same holds for ideas, skills, and contributions in the workplace. Employees must recognize their responsibility for the way they present their gifts; if they don't, we have a responsibility to teach them. It's not just about what you bring to the table but how you bring it. Your presentation, your attitude, and the context in which you offer your contribution can significantly impact how it's received.

BY RECEIVING GIFTS PROPERLY, YOU INCREASE YOUR BOUNTY

A leader's ability to recognize, value, and appropriately respond to the contributions of team members is a fundamental skill, one that is vital for a positive and productive work environment. Remember, the gifts you receive don't consist only of what they directly provide but also of the effort, thought, and intention behind them.

In my years of leading teams, I've come to see that receiving gifts—whether they be contributions, ideas, or efforts—is at the heart of creating a thriving work environment. The right atmosphere can make or break the success of an organization, and understanding this connection is crucial for any leader seeking to build a vibrant, dynamic, and successful team. In our next chapter, we'll delve into the precise ways you can craft this atmosphere to facilitate innovation, collaboration, and collective success.

3

THE ATMOSPHERE YOU CREATE

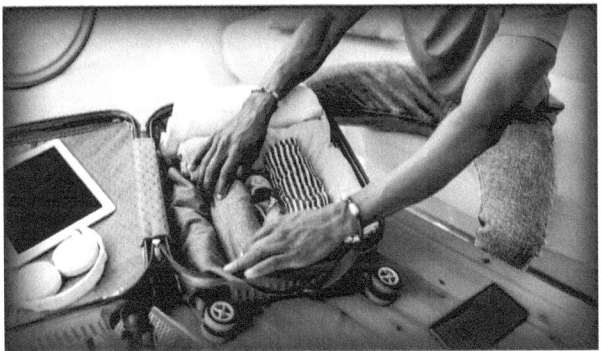

Source: Elevated Leadership

Before we begin this chapter, I want you to do something for me. Close your eyes and imagine the feeling of anticipation and other emotions you experience right before a long-awaited vacation. Picture every element: the excitement as you cross each day off the calendar, the joy of sharing plans with friends and family, the vivid daydreams of the experiences that await. Do you feel that energy? This type of anticipation can be a powerful motivator, infusing us with a sense of drive even in the most exhausting circumstances. What if you could foster this same sense of anticipation within the workplace? It's not as far-fetched as it might seem. The key lies in creating the right atmosphere and environment.

Creating an environment that offers new and engaging experiences can transform a team's outlook. If you can get your team to come to work not just out of obligation but with anticipation, their productivity and overall morale will skyrocket. It can also enhance your own personal passion and energy levels. I learned this firsthand, and I can sum up my experience with a quick story about a long-awaited vacation.

A few years ago, my wife and I were preparing to take a trip to a resort in Mexico, something we had been anticipating for a long time. We were looking forward to an adventure, not to mention some well-earned time off. However, as the day grew nearer, we were still dealing with work obligations and projects. On the last day before our vacation, we were both busy all day, and I ended up working late. When we finally got home, we were completely wiped out. The worst part was we still had all of our packing to do.

Now, if this had been a regular day, we would have said enough is enough, ordered takeout, and sat down on the couch. But we started talking about the resort: the sun-drenched beaches, our hotel suite overlooking the ocean, and the exotic food and drink. All of this was waiting for us, and the mere thought of these future blessings ignited our sense of motivation. One moment we were tired, and the next moment, wired; suddenly we had an abundance of ambition and got everything ready in seemingly no time at all. Before we knew it, we were on those beautiful beaches we had been dreaming about for so long, all thanks to that last-second burst of energy.

That's what's so powerful about anticipation: it can *create* energy all on its own, motivating individuals in even the most draining circumstances. That's why developing a work environment that people feel excited about is so important. If the atmosphere of your organization is both functional and inspiring, you can attain the levels of productivity and morale you desire. Not only that, but you can ensure that everyone isn't just working to work; they're working to build something together. To do this, you first need to understand the thought processes of the individuals who enter your workspace.

GROUP PSYCHOLOGY, TEAM DYNAMICS, AND OPTIMIZED WORKSPACES

Before you create anticipation, it's important to consider what it means to have "your own space." Many people lack a space that they feel is truly their own. Sure, we have our homes, but in many cases, we sacrifice much of this space to make our children and spouses happy. Despite this sacrifice, it's inherent to human nature to want a place we can call our own. Recognizing this psychological desire gives leaders the unique opportunity to fulfill an unmet need. By transforming physical spaces in a way that resonates with individual personality and work style, we can foster the sense of personal ownership and pride our teams are looking for.

To understand what kind of changes you need to make, start by engaging in meaningful dialogue with team members. Try to truly understand who they are, discover what they aspire to achieve, and align these aspirations with the physical design of their workspace. The information you gather will guide you in ensuring that every physical aspect—from the layout to the decor—mirrors these personal and professional aspirations.

It's also important to remember that these physical features can play a pivotal role in team dynamics. A well-arranged workspace can encourage collaboration, creativity, and a sense of belonging. By intentionally designing work areas with group and collective identity in mind, you ensure that your team feels supported and valued while contributing toward common goals. These changes can vary greatly; some examples are ergonomic workstations for physical comfort, communal areas for social interaction, and recreational spaces for employees to take a break and avoid burnout.

Whatever changes you make, ensure that they are not just superficial adjustments intended to make an area "look good." Designing an atmosphere is more about meaningful transformations that resonate with the core of your team's needs and your organization's goals. If you take your time when making these adjustments, you send a powerful message to each and every person in your organization: They matter. Not only that, but research indicates that strategically designing your work environment can boost motivation and productivity, enhance team cohesion, and elevate employee satisfaction.

In a 2022 study, researchers found that an encouraging and supportive work environment significantly influences employee performance. In addition, the right environment can bolster employees' commitment, enhance their drive to achieve, and amplify their overall productivity.[2]

This study underpins a belief I've championed for years: the environment we create as leaders is the bedrock on which we build success. It's the soil in which we sow the seeds of commitment and excellence. Our job is to craft a space where our teams thrive, their skills are recognized and utilized, and their dedication to our shared vision is nurtured.

THE IDEAL WORK ENVIRONMENT

The power of a thoughtfully designed workplace is something I've seen time and time again throughout my career. Take, for instance, a company in Waterloo, Iowa, that I had the pleasure of working with. They transformed their entrance with a bold message: "Enter motivated." As employees left, another message above the door read, "Leave inspired." This

---

[2] Gu Zhenjing, Supat Chupradit, Kuo Yen Ku, Abdelmohsen A. Nassani, and Mohamed Haffar, "Impact of Employees' Workplace Environment on Employees' Performance: A Multi-Mediation Model," *Frontiers in Public Health* 10 (2022): 890400, https://doi.org/10.3389/fpubh.2022.890400.

simple yet profound change in their physical space invigorated their entire atmosphere and aligned perfectly with their new vision to "change the world, one mind at a time." You could see the shift in each employee's demeanor as they walked past those signs. They weren't just there to cross some t's and dot some i's anymore; they were there to help make that vision a reality.

We can see the effect of environmental changes in company offices all over the world. Take Google, a titan in the tech industry. There are over 1,300 micro-kitchens within Google's global offices (which total around seventy). These kitchens don't only help keep employees well fed and make them feel like work is their second home; they serve as a hub for creativity and collaboration. Each micro-kitchen encourages random interactions, meaning this design choice embodies Google's philosophy that great ideas can spring from the most casual encounters. It's an atmosphere that speaks to the very heart of innovation, turning the simple act of making a cup of coffee into an opportunity for creative exchange and problem-solving.

Another inspiring example comes from the California headquarters of Pixar Animation Studios. The central atrium, originally designed as a mere space to house mailboxes, was transformed by Pixar and Apple cofounder Steve Jobs. He envisioned the space as a bustling crossroads where the company's artists, tech specialists, and writers could meet and converse outside their isolating offices. To further spark their passion, artwork from Pixar's films adorns the walls of the atrium, serving as a constant reminder of their collective achievements and the magic they create. It's not just a building; it's a living canvas that tells the story of the company's journey, challenges, and triumphs.

While these transformations aren't just about aesthetics, they do play a significant role. Imagine walking into a workspace that not only is visually pleasing but also radiates a sense of purpose and enthusiasm. Think about the tactile nature of it, how it looks, how your senses are engaged. Does the space smell good? What sounds fill the air? Are there visual cues that align with the company's goals and values? Each of these elements plays a vital role in shaping your team's day-to-day experience.

The impact of an environment can be palpable, but unfortunately that impact isn't always positive. If you walk into a cluttered, dirty, foul-smelling place of business, your expectations will drop to the floor. *Why would anyone spend their money here?*

you would think as you shut the door behind you. Now, that's just the customer's perspective; how do you think the employees feel when they walk into that building every day? In many cases, you can tell right away when a place is not functioning correctly, and in my experience, the fault usually lies with the leadership.

But let's say instead you walk into an immaculate business: light music is playing, there's a pleasant scent in the air, and they've neatly displayed their products in tidy display cases. How do you think the employees will look? In these situations, they will almost always appear smiling, happy, and genuinely excited to help you. These environments exude success, and that feeling affects everyone who enters—employee and customer alike. This principle doesn't apply only to businesses, either. Any organization can benefit from an honest analysis and alteration of its work environment.

HOW DO I CREATE THIS KIND OF ENVIRONMENT?

Now that we've established the psychology behind creating the right space and what these areas should look like, let's talk about the practical aspects of building these environments. Your approach will vary based on your industry and team composition, but there are universal principles that can guide you in enhancing your workplace to foster anticipation and engagement. Here are a few I consider whenever I'm looking to change the physical attributes of a workspace.

Functional Design
Each area of the workplace should have a clear purpose. Designate spaces for collaboration, quiet individual work, informal gatherings, and relaxation. Ensure you equip these areas with the necessary tools and technology. For instance, collaboration zones could have whiteboards and projectors, while individual work areas might have noise-canceling options. These functional designs, while serving specific purposes, also contribute to the overall atmosphere by creating spaces where employees can work optimally.

Metamorphic Spaces
The workplace should be a dynamic area that constantly evolves to prevent monotony. Redesign office spaces, introduce thematic elements that change with seasons or company milestones, and create dedicated sites for creativity, learning, and communication. Use scientific concepts like color theory to influence certain moods: blue, for example, can

help to foster focus and concentration, while red or orange can help to stimulate creativity and energy. Employees will look forward to these responsive and vibrant changes like they would anticipate any other exciting experience.

Health and Safety
Prioritize a healthy environment by ensuring good air quality, proper lighting, and cleanliness. Consider air purifiers, ample natural light, and natural cleaning schedules. Ensure that the workspace complies with all safety regulations, and overall seek to produce a secure and comfortable environment for everyone.

Regular Feedback and Collaboration
Establish channels for regular feedback from your team about their workspace. This could be through surveys, suggestion boxes, or regular meetings dedicated to workspace improvement. Encourage openness and honesty in these discussions. By understanding team members' needs and preferences, you can make informed decisions about the design and functionality of the workspace.

Focusing on these aspects will allow you to do more than just construct a place to work. You'll shape an environment that resonates with your organization's ethos. Such a space not only enhances productivity and well-being but also becomes a living representation of your organization's principles and aspirations. It's in these thoughtfully crafted spaces that our core values find tangible expression, our culture takes root and grows, and we foster a sense of community. These three elements—core values, culture, and community—can be the building blocks of both your organization and the environments within it.

THE THREE CS: Core Values, Culture, and Community

In my years of leadership experience, I've found that the most successful organizational environments are built on three primary pillars. I call these the Three Cs: Core Values, Culture, and Community. To round out our chapter, let's take a look at each of these pillars and at how your environments should represent them.

Core Values

Our core values are our compass; they guide every one of our decisions and actions in our daily lives. I shared some of my core values with you in the introduction to this book: being people-centered, being growth-minded, and being driven to empower. However, your values may differ depending on your unique goals, the nature of your organization, and your vision for the future. Your workspace should be a physical representation of your organization's core values. For example, if innovation is a core value, the workspace should have areas designed to inspire creativity and out-of-the-box thinking, like brainstorming rooms or innovation labs. On the other hand, if sustainability is a value, this could be reflected in an organization's use of eco-friendly design choices and materials.

Culture

Culture is the way these core values manifest—it's how we bring these abstract concepts to life in the everyday actions and decisions of our organization.

Much like it does for your core values, your workspace should also serve as a manifestation of your organization's culture. For instance, if you have a culture that values transparency and openness, glass walls and open spaces can reinforce these principles. If your culture emphasizes wellness and work-life balance, include a wellness center or relaxation zone in your workplace design.

Community

Putting our core values and culture to the test means seeing how they extend to both the community within our organization and the community we serve. Designing your workspace to foster a sense of community will involve focusing on areas that allow for interaction, specifically your organization's communal spaces. Some will be for team members, like cafeterias, lounges, or even outdoor areas where individuals can gather informally. Others will be for meeting clients or community members, like open reception areas or community meeting rooms. Such spaces encourage interaction and help build not only stronger internal bonds but stronger connections to the wider community.

Each element of your workspace should resonate with the Three Cs. This holistic approach ensures that your physical environment is more than just an assembly line for products or a purveyor of services; it's a reflection of your organization's image, a breeding ground for innovation, and a community hub.

THE ATMOSPHERE YOU CREATE IS ESSENTIAL

Our environment sets the tone for everything, including how our team members interact, what they accomplish, and how they tackle challenges. It's a powerful force that shapes behaviors and attitudes. The onus is on us, as leaders, to consciously mold these spaces. The physical environment we create should embody our core values, nurture our culture, and extend our organization's influence on our internal and external communities. When we get it right, we're not just building a workplace but creating a microcosm of the world we believe should exist—collaborative, productive, and deeply human.

But the right environment only goes so far, especially when it comes to the challenges that leaders and employees face on the long road to success. In our next chapter, we'll look at some examples of major roadblocks that you may encounter, their root causes, and the best ways to prevent them from slowing you down.

4
ROADBLOCKS

Image by Tyler Scheviak on Unsplash

I want you to picture a winding path leading up a mountain. The trail is well worn but surrounded by craggy cliffs, and you're guiding a group carefully higher and higher. You turn a corner and suddenly find that a large pile of rocks has completely blocked your way. What is your first instinct?

You likely want to clear the path as quickly as possible, not considering how those rocks came to be there but focusing on simply moving forward. You and your group clear the rubble, but you hear a rumble on the mountainside as you move through. More rocks are falling. Not only is your path blocked once again, but now your group is split and you have lost members.

Roadblocks aren't just hurdles that need to be cleared; they're opportunities to learn, grow, and strengthen the bonds within our teams. Instead of simply removing them, we have to understand their root cause. That way, we can learn to anticipate them and, most importantly, transform them into gateways to future prosperity. Mind you, roadblocks will still occur, and mistakes will still happen; they're a natural part of life. But as a leader, you need to be forgiving, willing to offer counsel, and ready to coach your team to ensure better outcomes in the future.

UNEARTHING THE ROOTS OF A ROADBLOCK

Many of the roadblocks we face start small, like a minor patch of weeds in a garden. But much like weeds, if the roots of these roadblocks are ignored, they will spread until we're completely overwhelmed. To address them, you can't just apply a quick fix. Much like cutting off the top of a weed won't stop it from growing back, a temporary solution to a serious roadblock will mean larger problems later. Instead, you have to attack a problem at its source.

While the nature of a specific roadblock can take any number of forms, I find that many of these problems grow from seven main roots: tradition, communication breakdown, leadership tunnel vision, long-tenured employees, fear of investing, pride, and a lack of accountability.

Root #1: Tradition

To understand how tradition can cause problems, let's look at a hypothetical situation. A young entrepreneur recently inherited his family's company. This company had been in business for decades, operating primarily based on the ingrained traditions of his family. But as the entrepreneur grew up, he saw the world around him changing. Still, his family insists that the old ways are better, claiming they are "the way things have always been done." Despite their conviction, the entrepreneur has a feeling that without adaptation, their company will be left behind. He faces a dilemma: should he honor tradition or embrace innovation?

I've seen this type of roadblock in a variety of long-standing businesses, and in some ways, I understand the line of thinking that leads to this problem. You've heard the old adage "If it ain't broke, don't fix it." As catchy as the saying is, it isn't always true. Past performance does not guarantee future results, and if tradition is starting to slow the wheels of progress, then what isn't broken now may be sooner than you think.

To address this roadblock root, you have to get your organization prepared to venture outside its comfort zone. While new methods and ideas may be scary, they can also be exciting. Instead of focusing on the destruction of traditions, build up your team's anticipation of what's to come. Face that fear of the unknown head-on and fight the innate resistance to change that often plagues human nature. Use case studies and statistics to illustrate why new methods may be effective, and slowly introduce these concepts into your operations. That way, your teams have time to adjust while also being able to see the direct effect of each new change.

Root #2: Communication Breakdown
Anyone who's been in the middle of a communication breakdown knows it can be fertile ground for numerous issues. I remember one organization I worked with where communication had deteriorated so significantly that silence had become the norm. Organizational members held ideas close to their chest, and management only superficially acknowledged any concerns that were raised. In some cases they ignored them completely. This wasn't just a situation where apathy had taken hold—it was a space where open communication, whether on purpose or by accident, had been stifled completely.

Looking at the situation, I quickly realized that the silence had nothing to do with a lack of ideas. In fact, the team members I talked with had plenty of insights and suggestions that could have propelled the organization forward. The issue was they didn't feel comfortable expressing these ideas. The fear of judgment or reprisal silenced voices that should have been leading the charge for change and innovation. It was an atmosphere where the status quo reigned supreme, not because that's what worked best, but because it was the path of least resistance.

To repair this broken chain of communication, I had to start a dialogue. We reshaped team meetings to be more inclusive, crowdsourcing ideas rather than trickling them down from the top. We established feedback channels and encouraged leaders to respond constructively to new ideas. Over time we built trust, and team members began to feel their contributions were valued. By the time I finished my work, the silence had been replaced with a constant exchange of ideas. Instead of a loose collection of individuals working in isolation, the organization felt like a collaborative unit that could draw on the full power of its resources to accomplish its goals.

Root #3: Leadership Tunnel Vision
Tunnel vision plagues a majority of leaders at one time or another. Many of these leaders are acting in good faith, focusing on the culmination of their vision or the overarching goals of their organization. However, by staring so intently at the horizon, they miss what's happening all around them. People, problems, and day-to-day activities may fall to the wayside as a leader stays glued to their telescope, eyes locked on the stars.

This tunnel vision can manifest in a variety of ways and can directly affect an organization's workforce. Teams that focus solely on large-scale goals can be efficient but also devoid of an essential sense of humanity. A well-oiled machine is still a machine, and team members may begin to feel that their individual efforts are lost to the greater grinding of your organization's gears. After a while, what once seemed like an unstoppable train of productivity will begin to slow. The worst part is that those afflicted with leadership tunnel vision may not even notice until it's too late. They may focus on what's to come while failing to notice that, without a course correction, those events may not come at all.

To address leadership tunnel vision, take a step back from the telescope. Engage in meaningful dialogues with employees, not just about what they are accomplishing but about how they feel and how their lives outside of work are going. Celebrate successes, pull lessons out of failures, and recognize individual contributions. By doing this, you create a balance between the group and the individual and maintain an essential 360-degree view of what's happening around you.

Root #4: Long-Tenured Employees
While long-tenured employees are often significant and valuable assets, they can also be a root of many roadblocks. These individuals may have been with your organization since its inception and, over time,

could have lost their passion or willingness to strive for accomplishment.

One of the major patterns that these employees fall into is complacency. Much like other roadblocks, complacency in an organization can grow slowly over time. In many cases it starts out innocently, more as a comfort with protocol than as actual negligence. But as people become too comfortable, shortcuts can begin to happen. Inevitably this will lead someone to cut a corner that can't be easily repaired.

Long-tenured employees can also be incredibly resistant to change. They may look at the latest ideas with skepticism, preferring the safety of the known over the uncertainty of innovation. Because these individuals carry influence, this type of thinking may begin to spread throughout your organization's culture, reducing your other team members' abilities to adapt and grow.

When making changes in organizations with numerous entrenched employees, the key is to take it slow. Rapid change is often met with resistance and even hostility. As leaders, we have to shift things gradually, seek regular feedback, and include longtime employees in the decision-making process. This approach will not only ease transitions but allow you to leverage the experience and knowledge of tenured employees for your organization's benefit.

Root #5: Fear of Investing
Another root problem I've seen is the hesitancy some leaders display when it comes to their employees' development. This hesitation often stems from the fear that employees, once developed and skilled, may leave the organization and take their newly honed ability to competitors or to their own new ventures.

While this fear is understandable, it can also significantly impede an organization's growth and development. When leaders withhold opportunities for growth, training, or professional development, they are inadvertently creating a stagnant environment. Employees begin to feel unchallenged and undervalued, which decreases morale and productivity. If this goes on too long, the fear that they will leave becomes a self-fulfilling prophecy as they depart to find greener pastures.

To combat this fear, you have to shift your perspective from the possibility of loss to the potential for mutual growth. Investing in employees' growth can lead to numerous benefits for the organization, including increased innovation, higher job satisfaction, and a stronger, more competent workforce. Not only that, but you'll actually build loyalty, not lose it. In most cases, employees who grow with an organization are more committed to its success.

Root #6: Pride
Pride is a difficult roadblock to assess because a certain level of pride is not only healthy but necessary. You should take pride in your vision and in the work your teams are accomplishing; however, we've all heard the saying "too much of a good thing." An overabundance of pride isn't about healthy self-respect or a sense of accomplishment but an overinflated sense of self-importance that places the leader at the center of the organizational universe. This type of pride is built on the belief that, because of their position at the top of the organizational chart, a leader is somehow inherently superior or infallible.

In leadership, excessive pride can manifest as a reluctance to listen to others, a dismissal of subordinates' ideas, and a rigid adherence to one's own methods and strategies. This roadblock can share similarities with the challenges presented by tradition, except the source is entirely the leaders themselves. Prideful leaders believe their way is the only way to go and dismiss others' contributions as inferior. Their mindset is organizational poison, stifling innovation and growth while breeding resentment and disengagement within the team.

To overcome this roadblock, leaders must first recognize and acknowledge its presence. This requires a strong sense of self-awareness and humility that may take time to achieve. Leaders who find themselves ensnared in the pride trap are often looking through the lens of a top-down hierarchy. Step one is to shift this perspective and view the organization as a whole. Leaders will also need to acknowledge that their role is not just to assert authority but to harness the collective intelligence and strength of their team.

By removing this roadblock, leaders can transform from commanding overseers into facilitators of collective growth. It's about evolving from a position of "command and control" to one of "inspire and empower." Through such an evolution, you can revitalize the health of your organization and create sustainable success that is achievable only through group collaboration.

Root #7: A Lack of Accountability

A lack of accountability at the leadership level is a subtle yet pervasive roadblock I've seen throughout my career. One reason this issue is often overlooked is because it's taking place at the highest levels of an organization, so in many ways, the only ones who can change it are those taking part.

For example, let's imagine a tech startup with a brilliant CEO. This person has a clear vision, one that could revolutionize their industry, but they also have a significant flaw: a lack of accountability. Their ideas are groundbreaking, but their follow-through is lackluster. They may inspire their team initially, but as deadlines are missed and promises are broken, the team becomes discontented. The CEO's lack of accountability not only stalls projects but erodes the trust and morale of the team.

So why does this happen? As high-status individuals in the organization, leaders are inadvertently placed above the accountability structures that keep a workforce on track. They set goals, assign tasks, and evaluate performance, but who evaluates them and their performance? If the buck stops with them, then who can ensure they follow through on their commitments?

One effective solution to this roadblock is to establish an external advisory board. These boards are given authority to hold the CEO accountable, ask tough questions, and ensure follow-through on commitments. Regular meetings are set up with the

CEO or leadership team to gather progress reports, tackle challenges, and hear feedback.

A culture of accountability starts at the top; when a leader models accountability, it sets the tone for the entire organization. This kind of company culture encourages everyone to take ownership of their work, leading to a more engaged, motivated, and productive team.

TURNING ROADBLOCKS INTO GATEWAYS: Eight Practical Tips

While your roadblocks may not fit a cookie-cutter mold, some general guidelines and techniques can help you turn impediments into successes. Here are eight ways you can prevent roadblocks and their roots from taking hold or stopping your organization from moving forward.

1. Embrace Change and Encourage Innovation

Traditional methods may have brought your organization this far, but they might not carry you into the future. Encourage team members to think freely and be open to current ideas. Remember, innovation is not just about tremendous changes; sometimes small tweaks can lead to significant improvements.

2. Foster Open Communication

Establishing a culture in which team members feel safe to voice their opinions and ideas is essential. You can do this in a variety of ways, including through regular team meetings, suggestion boxes, and open-door policies. Encourage open dialogue by actively listening to your teams, which can ensure they know their input is considered valuable.

3. Balance Vision with Awareness

Vision is important, and as a leader, you need to focus on long-term goals. However, you can't lose sight of the present. Regularly check in with your team, acknowledge their hard work, and be aware of the dynamics within your organization. A balanced approach ensures that you keep moving toward your goals without overlooking day-to-day operations.

4. Leverage Long-Tenured Employees

While they might resist change, long-tenured employees are often reservoirs of knowledge and experience. Involve them in the decision-making process, especially when there will be changes to familiar processes. Their insights can be invaluable, and their involvement can help to ease organizational transitions for the entire team.

5. Cultivate a Culture of Accountability

Accountability trickles down from the top, and leaders have to be role models for teams to have a blueprint for proper conduct. Acknowledge your mistakes and show your team that accountability isn't about blame but about learning and improving.

6. Address the Fear of Employee Departure

While you may still have anxiety about potentially losing a well-trained employee, it can't stop you from helping them realize their potential. A nurtured employee is an asset even if they move on. Their growth contributes to your organization's legacy and reputation. Moreover, investing in people often leads to greater loyalty and a stronger team.

7. Regularly Reassess and Adjust Strategies

The business world is dynamic, and what works today might not work tomorrow. Regularly reassess your strategies, be open to feedback, and be willing to adjust your approach. Agility can be the key to navigating through and overcoming roadblocks.

8. Celebrate Successes and Learn from Failures

Recognize your teams when they overcome a roadblock, as it can help boost morale and motivate them to continue excelling. When a roadblock proves challenging, you can ensure it's used as a learning opportunity instead of seen as a failure. Analyze the root of the problem, discuss the particulars with your team, and use these insights to improve.

BRIDGING THE GAP: Roadblocks and Leadership Barriers

While external roadblocks can impede an organization's success, sometimes the barriers lie closer than you think: directly between you and your full potential as a leader. To helm an organization with maximum efficacy, you must look within and address the introspective aspects of leading. In our next chapter, we'll look at a few of these leadership challenges, including pride, self-centeredness, overemphasis on deadlines, and a lack of empathy. You'll learn how to become the captain of a ship that everyone wants to board, not because they have to but because they believe in their leader and the destination.

5
BARRIERS TO LEADERSHIP

Image by Erik Mclean on Unsplash

In guiding leaders toward a more effective approach, I often emphasize a crucial principle:

Figure out why you do what you do.

It's not enough to know that your methods are effective; you also need to understand *why* they work if you want to replicate those results in the future. To understand this concept, you have to recognize and confront the barriers blocking your full potential as a leader. This is not just about simple troubleshooting; it's about gaining profound insight into our own leadership style and the factors that influence it.

To accomplish this, leaders need to develop a keen sense of introspection. While it's important to have a clear vision and set your sights on future goals, being aware of obstacles that could impede these aspirations is equally crucial. True leadership transcends the mere crafting of an inspiring vision; it requires actively identifying and addressing the challenges that might obstruct the vision's realization. This process is a critical aspect of leadership development, requiring not just an acknowledgment of these barriers but a deep understanding of their nature and the reasons you must overcome them.

UNDERSTANDING THE IMPORTANCE OF OVERCOMING BARRIERS

The path to optimal leadership is beset by internal and external challenges, and in many cases, we create these challenges for ourselves. Fortunately, we have the power to destroy these barriers using the combined strength of introspection and self-awareness. Ask yourself, "Why do I make the decisions I do? What drives my leadership style?" By taking the time to discern the answers to these and other introspective questions, you set the stage for significant personal development. This, in turn, leads to team growth.

Many leaders gravitate toward their comfort zones, unknowingly fostering environments that lack challenge and fail to maximize team potential. It's a natural inclination to seek comfort, yet it's a tendency that can hamper growth. Your comfort zone, a realm often invisibly shaped by unrecognized biases, needs critical examination and active effort to expand. This process will require honesty, vulnerability, and a commitment to continuous self-improvement.

In developing self-awareness, we also nurture our empathy and emotional intelligence—crucial tools for inspiring and motivating those around us. By stepping into another person's shoes and trying to understand their perspective, we can foster individual growth, bolster team cohesion, and boost overall productivity. It all starts with self-reflection: dedicating time to introspectively identifying the barriers you've erected and the underlying assumptions influencing your decisions. Recognizing and addressing these foundational elements is key to your leadership evolution.

CRITICAL QUESTIONS FOR SELF-EVALUATION

One of the core components of leadership growth is self-evaluation. This typically means asking yourself challenging questions to uncover areas where you can improve. I've crafted a set of questions to prompt deep reflection and actionable insights. As you ponder each question, I encourage you to think of specific instances and examples that illustrate your answers, thereby creating a more vivid and actionable portrait of your leadership style.

- What are my core values, and how do they influence my leadership style?
- What feedback have I received that I might have dismissed too quickly?
- How do my biases and assumptions affect my decision-making?
- How well do I understand the motivations and aspirations of my team members?
- What steps am I taking to foster a positive and inclusive work environment?

- In what ways have I demonstrated emotional intelligence in difficult situations?
- How do I react to failure, both my own and my team's?
- What am I doing to encourage continuous learning and growth in myself and others?

After answering these questions, keep your responses in a place where you can revisit them. Periodic reflection, say every six months, can help you track your progress and adapt your leadership style. Also, consider sharing some of these questions with trusted colleagues or your team to gain external perspectives.

Ultimately, the goal is not just to answer these questions once but to engage with them regularly as part of your leadership evolution. This practice, coupled with a commitment to act on the insights you gain, will propel you toward more effective, empathetic, and dynamic leadership.

IDENTIFYING BIAS AND OVERCOMING PERSONAL OBSTACLES

One difficult fact to face is that we navigate daily life with a set of biases—it's an intrinsic part of being human. However, it's crucial not to view these biases as personal failings but as natural tendencies of the human mind. Our brains are judgment machines hardwired to make quick judgments and categorize information, an ancient survival mechanism that now aids us in modern decision-making. This instinctive search for patterns and familiarity is a double-edged sword; while often helpful, it can inadvertently lead us to biases that cloud our judgment, particularly in complex situations requiring informed and impartial decisions. Recognizing and understanding these biases is the first step toward ensuring they don't unconsciously influence our choices and interactions.

To dismantle internal biases, you'll need to develop strategies to increase self-awareness. There are several methods to achieve this; journaling is a particularly effective technique.

By dedicating time each day to record and reflect on your thoughts, decisions, and interactions, you isolate a small part of your day specifically for introspection and self-examination. Use your journal as a tool to delve into the reasons behind your actions and decisions. By consistently engaging in this reflective process, you encourage a mindset that actively seeks out and considers diverse perspectives, challenging your default assumptions and broadening your understanding.

Proactively seeking feedback is another excellent way to challenge and overcome assumptive thought patterns. Engage with your team members, asking for their input on various decisions and methods. When soliciting feedback, focus not only on the practical aspects but also on the emotional impact of your decisions. You can accomplish this through structured feedback sessions, anonymous surveys, or open forums, encouraging candid and comprehensive responses. This practice won't just inform your decisions; it will also enhance your emotional intelligence and social awareness, which can further break down any barriers created by personal biases.

As you progressively shed layers of bias, your focus will naturally expand beyond yourself. Often, even before you consciously direct your efforts outward, you may observe a positive shift in your workplace culture as a direct result of your internal growth. This transformation is characterized by a tangible increase in positivity and inclusivity within your team, reflecting a leadership style that clearly values diverse perspectives.

You can further build on these elements by actively promoting an atmosphere of respect and inclusion. Set clear expectations for behavior and communication, celebrate diversity, and foster a sense of belonging among all your team members. Provide opportunities for open dialogue on every operational level, allowing team members to share their ideas and experiences with each other and with those in leadership.

Maintaining vigilance against biases is an ongoing commitment essential for effective leadership. These ingrained thought patterns can resurface subtly and unexpectedly, so managing them requires constant attention and effort. It's important to establish regular practices that encourage bias awareness, such as periodic reviews of decision-making processes or diversity training. An inclusive environment where every team member feels genuinely valued and understood is not just a moral imperative but a strategic advantage. Such settings empower individuals to contribute their unique gifts and operate at peak performance levels.

FIVE COMMON BARRIERS AND THEIR SOLUTIONS

In my years of navigating the complex landscape of leadership, I've come across recurring challenges that seem to emerge regardless of industry or organization. These impediments and biases aren't just abstract concepts but real issues that can significantly affect our ability to effectively lead. Let's take a look at five common barriers I've seen in my leadership career, paired with their potential solutions.

Barrier #1: Team-Selection Bias

Challenge

Leaders might unconsciously or inadvertently choose team members who share the same background, experience, or perspective as theirs. This inclination, though seemingly benign, can lead to the creation of a homogeneous team. While such a team might operate harmoniously, the lack of diversity in viewpoints can result in an echo chamber, significantly limiting the team's potential for creativity and innovation.

Solution

Implement a more structured and objective recruitment process that seeks to include diverse viewpoints. You can also involve individuals with different perspectives in the team assembly process. By taking these steps, you'll enrich project conversations and create a more inclusive workplace culture.

Barrier #2: Leadership-Oriented Environment

Challenge

Some leaders will create a work environment that suits their own likes and dislikes without first considering the needs of their team members. This can manifest in various aspects of the workplace, ranging from the physical setup and aesthetic to more subtle elements like the organizational culture, communication styles, and decision-making processes. In these environments, team members feel as though they have no value in their organization, which reduces their anticipation of the future and dampens their productivity.

Solution

Conduct surveys or hold meetings specifically designed to address the work environment. When assembling teams to draft and implement changes, it's vital to consider a wide range of perspectives. Be open to experimentation during transitional periods, as some changes may not work or could take time to show results. Check in with team members regularly to see whether environmental changes are supporting their productivity and well-being.

Barrier #3: Overemphasis on Deadlines and Schedules

Challenge

Leaders often place strong emphasis on meeting deadlines and adhering to strict schedules, viewing them as key indicators of efficiency and success. While time management is undoubtedly crucial, an overemphasis on deadlines can create a high-pressure environment. This type of atmosphere breeds burnout and leads to a decreased quality of work. Deadline pressure can also lead to a culture that values the end result more than the process or people involved, which can decimate team morale and dramatically reduce employee retention rates.

Solution
Start by setting realistic goals. Deadline crunches are often due to poor planning and a lack of foresight from those up top. By making a plan ahead of time, you can set a reasonable schedule that reduces stress and increases quality. Spread responsibilities evenly, as this can allow team members to manage their workload more effectively and prevent burnout. In addition, you'll want to build in schedule flexibility from the start, as some project aspects—particularly creative elements—cannot be rushed.

Barrier #4: Self-Centered Perspective

Challenge
Self-centered leaders may hyperfocus on their own goals, an approach that can create a disconnect between the leader and team members. Self-centric perspectives typically fail to consider the unique aspirations, motivations, and perspectives within the group; consequently, a lack of engagement and even resistance can occur in team members. A leader's

perspective, while important, shouldn't overshadow the collective vision and goals of the team.

Solution

Leaders who find themselves trapped in these mindsets need to make a concerted effort to connect with team members. Hold meetings specifically tailored to discuss the goals and challenges of your team. You can also have one-on-one discussions to personalize this approach and get the individual perspective of each member. In addition, it may be beneficial to have anonymous avenues for feedback, like surveys or suggestion boxes. These can allow team members to share their true feelings without the potential discomfort of identification.

Barrier #5: Micromanagement and Delegation Deficiency

Challenge

Leaders can inadvertently become obstacles, hindering both their own progress and that of their team. Two major manifestations of this are micromanagement and a lack of delegation. Micromanagement happens when leaders demand inclusion in every detail of a project, insisting that their methods are the only ones that work. A lack of delegation can go hand-in-hand with this, as a leader may believe they are the only one who can complete certain tasks. When combined, these tendencies to control can lead to decision-making bottlenecks, reduced morale, and a lack of initiative among team members.

Solution
To get out of both your own way and your employees' way, you'll want to foster a culture of trust. Embrace delegation and give your team responsibility and autonomy to execute tasks. You won't need to look over their shoulder or hold their hand for every decision or activity. Provide clear direction by communicating your vision, goals, and expectations, then take a step back. While you'll still be nearby for guidance if necessary, giving your team members the reins can encourage them to develop professionally while allowing you to focus on executive-level tasks.

THE GREATEST BARRIER MAY BE DIFFICULT TO FACE

One of the most significant barriers to leadership sits all the way down at the foundation of your leadership journey: within your vision. I'll state this plain and simple: If I read your vision and it doesn't give me chills, I can guarantee that it won't inspire your teams. Your vision can't just be words on a page—it has to be a living, breathing embodiment of what you and your team aspire to achieve. We're talking about the genesis of your passion, the spark that will fuel your team's sense of anticipation for years to come.

If bureaucracy clouds your vision, or if it's hindered by the very structures meant to support it, then it becomes a barrier rather than a beacon. If red tape wraps your vision in procedural hurdles, passion will inevitably run dry. That is precisely why, in our leadership workshops, we dedicate considerable time to revisiting and revitalizing your vision, mission, and core values. These elements are the heart and soul of transformational leadership, and without them, you won't succeed.

Remember, your vision is a gift. When a person opens a gift, they feel that they matter, that they're important. If your employees aren't coming to work excited, then you aren't giving them anything to look forward to. These people need to feel that their work is more than just a job—they want to contribute to something meaningful, something that excites them and gives them a sense of purpose. The days of employees being satisfied with just having a "job" are long gone. Today, people want to be part of something bigger than themselves. Your vision can create that space, a grand show that they'll clamor to purchase a ticket for. If they don't, then you have to ask yourself: Are they the wrong employee, or are you the wrong leader?

OVERCOMING BARRIERS TO BUILD BRIDGES

Whether the barriers to our success are internal or external, they often get in the way of forming connections. Organizations thrive on the bridges and pathways that connect leaders and their teams, but these connecting structures aren't built by accident. In our next chapter, we'll look at the meaning of building bridges as a leader, the power of acknowledging mistakes, and the sustainable power of a constructive work environment.

THE BRIDGE AND THE APOLOGY

Image by Cody Hiscox on Unsplash

If you're exploring the concepts within this book, it's highly likely you are already leading a team or organization, and this is a stepping stone on your path to discovery and growth. It's also possible that, up until now, your leadership journey has lacked the guidance of the principles we've covered. If you've found value in what you've read and are considering integrating these insights into your leadership approach, you're at a pivotal moment—a moment that calls for a clear signal to your team that a new chapter is beginning for your organization.

In my years of guiding leaders through their development, I've found there's no tool more effective in marking this transition than a heartfelt apology. Now, the mere mention of the word *apology* may stir up feelings of defensiveness or resistance. You might be thinking, *Why should I apologize? How will this make me look?*

The truth is that the apology—much like everything else we've discussed—isn't about you. It's about your team, your collective goals, and the path you'll pave together into the future. The apology serves as a powerful moment of course correction, an acknowledgment that your vision is not just a continuation of the old ways but a paradigm shift, one that will steer your organization toward collaboration, empathy, and success.

You can think of the apology as a fine-tuned instrument designed to tear down the walls of defensiveness, misunderstanding, and resistance that may have been built up within your organization over time. By accepting responsibility and expressing vulnerability with a heartfelt apology, you are showing you're not perfect but something much better: you're human.

THE APOLOGY

I have found that apologies, more than almost any other leadership tool, have the profound ability to bridge the gaps created by past missteps. This realization dawned on me as I reflected on the countless interactions I've had with leaders across various industries. The power of an apology is not just in the expression of regret; it's in the formation of a connection. By mastering the art of apologizing, you can soften conversations and acknowledge past wrongs, ultimately leading to the establishment of common ground and long-lasting bridges.

An effective apology starts with a commitment to change and an acknowledgment of the impact of one's actions. The setting an apology occurs within may vary, with some more appropriate in group settings and others more effective when given one-on-one. Where you deliver an apology and what it contains will depend on the specific situation you face and the nature of the errors you need to address. I've provided a general example of an effective apology below.

> I've been reflecting on our time together recently, and I've come to a realization about my role as your leader: In my pursuit of our collective goals, I may have overlooked the individual contributions and needs you each have. I do not wish to overshadow your value as individuals or hinder your personal growth. It's clear now that in my pursuit of success, I have not been fully acknowledging the efforts and challenges you face daily.
>
> I want to say that this oversight is on me, and I am truly sorry for it. My intention was never to diminish your hard work or to make you feel undervalued. Looking ahead, I am committed to creating a more balanced and empathetic environment—one where your voices are heard, your well-being is prioritized, and your professional growth is given as much importance as our collective achievements.

> This apology is only the start. I promise to actively work on integrating your feedback into our decision-making processes, ensuring our goals reflect not only the company's aspirations but the aspirations and needs of every one of you. Together, let's shape a future in which we all thrive, not just as a team working toward common goals but as individuals with our own unique gifts, perspectives, and contributions.

Now, this is just a basic framework. You'll need to personalize your apology, ensuring that you take ownership of the past and set a clear direction for the future.

At the core of your statement should be the sincere desire to rectify your past mistakes. An organization's culture starts at the top, so any major change must begin with its leaders. Your apology should acknowledge this fact while also maintaining an underlying theme of humility and a commitment to learning.

Just like with vulnerability, many see an apology as an admission of weakness. Nothing could be further from the truth. An apology is an affirmation of our dedication to improvement as well as a way to show our employees that we recognize and value the time and effort they put toward our vision. This acknowledgment is the essence of bridge-building in leadership. With it, you'll be able to foster stronger connections with your team, understand their perspectives, and jointly navigate toward shared objectives.

BUILDING ON THE APOLOGY AND ESTABLISHING A NEW BASELINE FOR SUCCESS

The act of apologizing goes beyond merely saying words—it's a powerful gesture that resets the tone and expectations within an organization. By committing to a fresh way of leading, you lay the groundwork for a new phase of success, one in which open communication, mutual respect, and empathy are at the forefront. It's about shifting from a top-down, results-only focus to a more inclusive, team-oriented approach. Of course, this doesn't mean that results cease to be important; rather, it signifies a recognition that sustainable success is built on the foundation of a passionate, respected, and engaged workforce.

Once you've delivered your apology, the next step is to translate this new understanding into tangible actions and policies. These actions will likely involve revisiting company values, reassessing leadership approaches, and implementing new communication channels that encourage feedback and dialogue. In practical terms, it could mean more regular team meetings, one-on-one sessions to discuss career growth and personal development, and participation in leadership workshops that help to bolster your company's core values and mission. Your goal here is to show that the apology was sincere and that you (and your organization) are taking concrete steps toward change.

You'll be able to measure the efficacy of this approach not just in profits and deliverables but in team satisfaction, retention rates, and the overall health of your organization's culture. These metrics for success are far more sustainable, ethical, and attuned to the needs of the people who drive your organization forward.

Once you've seen tangible results, this will be your new baseline for success. From this foundation, you'll quickly see that the true power of an organization lies not just in its products or services but in its people and the values it upholds. We're talking about lasting prosperity, the kind that fosters innovation, loyalty, and a positive reputation both internally and externally. Your apology will pave the way for a leadership style that is more humane and effective while enriching the lives of those who can make your vision a reality.

THE IMPORTANCE AND IMPACT OF TOUGH CONVERSATIONS

A well-crafted apology and the establishment of viable bridges can liberate organization members from the shackles of fear and undue criticism. This shift can have a significant impact on individual well-being as well as on the health of your organization as a whole. Your apology will clearly show that you're not just about improving the bottom line but about supporting the people who work tirelessly to achieve your vision. This cultural change can transform an employee's experience from merely working for a paycheck to feeling like a valued member of a cohesive unit.

To ensure this impact occurs, you must be willing to have some tough conversations. Open dialogue is a key ingredient of growth, even when it includes criticism and other elements that are challenging. However, it's important to keep this criticism constructive. Personal attacks will be met with defensiveness and resistance that can erase any positive impact the apology may have had. You also want to ensure you are avoiding hypocrisy by addressing any uncomfortable truths about yourselves. For this to work, you'll have to put the needs of your team above your personal comfort. This act, while difficult, is a hallmark of true leadership.

By combining a willingness to engage in difficult conversations with a genuine apology, you'll receive levels of trust you've never seen before. Employees will no longer see you as simply "the boss" but as an approachable and understanding human being. Your workplace will become more authentic, issues will be addressed promptly, and solutions will be achieved collaboratively.

The transformation of a leadership style from authoritarian to empathic is not just about changing how we act but changing how employees feel. You have to erase the environmental traits that facilitate a culture of fear and emphasize the elements that foster trust. If the apology works as designed, you should end up with a safer, more respectful workplace, one that encourages honest communication and unrestrained contribution.

BRIDGE-BUILDING TO WIN SUSTAINABLY

The human brain loves the dopamine rush of a quick victory, but when it comes to constructing bridges, true success is defined by long-term sustainability. We don't always judge bridges by how quickly they can be traversed but by how long they can stand and how safely they ferry people to their destination. In many ways, the concept of bridge-building transcends the traditional metrics of "winning" and is anchored in the more holistic elements of team growth.

In addition to growth, the central focus here is the well-being of your employees. Successful organizations recognize that the value of their employees extends far beyond their immediate output. If you haven't already shifted your practices from a results-only focus to a people-centered ethos, you need to make it a priority. It could mean reassessing your core values, which is no easy task.

We've touched on core values throughout this book, and I've provided examples of ones I use to shape the organizations I lead. In addition to those previously mentioned values, several key principles I believe every organization needs are trust, respect, integrity, and an emphasis on teamwork—these are the building blocks for a sustainable work environment.

Empathy is another essential element, as it's one of the primary bridge-building materials. Once created, these empathy bridges can span the gap between employees and management. Members of your organization will be able to see decisions from your perspective, which will allow them to understand why you do what you do. Once your team has access to this bird's-eye view, you can transition to establishing strong shared goals.

USING YOUR BRIDGES: The Role of Goal-Setting

After you've laid the groundwork with an apology and started the process of bridge-building, goal-setting emerges as a crucial next step. Goal-setting is its own type of bridge construction in a way—the difference is that with goal-setting, you're bridging the gap between where your organization is now and where it aspires to be.

In the wake of the apology, setting goals becomes an act of reaffirmation and commitment to the new path carved out by the bridge-building process. Goals in this context are not just targets; they are the tangible expressions of change that the apology has initiated. They reflect the leader's commitment to acknowledging past shortcomings in order to actively work toward a better future.

The bridges you've built should also inform the goals you set; that way, they align with the aspirations of employees and the broader shared vision you've developed over time. This alignment is crucial for healing any past disconnects and moving forward in a unified direction. It's about ensuring that the goals set by the organization resonate with the team. This will help team members foster a sense of ownership and shared purpose.

Goal resonance is built on team empowerment. Members of your organization need to not only anticipate your organization's future but feel as though they have a say in the direction they're headed. Leaders can encourage these members by having them set personal goals that align with the organization's objectives. This will enhance their commitment and reinforce the trust and respect reestablished through the apology and bridge-building process.

Just as personal development is an ongoing process, so too is the maintenance of the bridges you've built with your teams. Regular and meaningful conversations about shared goals will be the cornerstone of this upkeep. These discussions act as "structural integrity checks," providing vital opportunities for feedback, adjustments, and recognition of progress. Maintaining a continuous dialogue allows you to sustain the movement you've generated with the apology, keep your team aligned, and ensure everyone remains focused on common goals. Through these efforts, the bridges you've built will not only stand firm but also strengthen over time, guiding your organization toward a shared horizon.

WHAT'S ON THE OTHER SIDE?

Apologizing and maintaining the bridges you've constructed won't be easy, but as with many of the recommendations I've made throughout this book, they're well worth it. Of course, it may be difficult to remember everything we've covered. Now that our time together is coming to a close, I want to revisit some key points from each chapter to help reinforce the main concepts and leave you with some parting advice on how to be the best leader you can as you move forward.

CONCLUSION

A recurring theme in this book is the fallibility of leaders, and in that same vein, I want to emphasize that our memory is not infallible either. It's perfectly understandable if you can't recall every insight I've shared throughout this book—the wisdom in these pages comes from years of experience and collaboration with numerous companies, and it can be a lot to take in. To make it easier to digest the information and find key facts when you need them later, I've summed up the main points of each chapter below.

CHAPTER 1: The Gifts You Give

In our opening chapter, we explored the transformative power of a leader's vision and its similarities to a gift of immense potential. We shouldn't hoard these gifts but rather share them with the world and the members of our organization. We can find the true power of our vision by exploring a key element of gift-giving: anticipation. To illustrate this, I shared a story of my wife Dawn's excitement surrounding opening Amazon packages, and how I inadvertently took away an opportunity for discovery by opening one of her boxes. It's important to create this same sense of anticipation and passion within our organizations; to do this, we must present our visions in the best way possible.

Chapter 1 explains how you can share your gifts by discussing a pivotal juncture at the start of any leadership role, what I call the "State of the Union moment." This is when you distill the past, present, and future of your organization, which I believe is best done by envisioning the process as the three components of a gift.

The Box: Where Your Organization Has Been
The first part of this process involves addressing your organization's history and acknowledging the achievements and actions of the leaders who preceded you. This is not the time to cast stones or criticize. Instead, show your appreciation for the work of your predecessors, your respect for past leadership, and your faith in your organization's legacy.

The Wrapping: Where Your Organization Is Now

Next, you'll need to evaluate your organization's current status. Discuss current strategies, where your organization is operating most effectively, and give progress reports on current projects. This is your chance to highlight your organization's strengths and weaknesses, showing where there is potential for future growth.

The Gift: Where Your Organization Will Be

The final part of this process is sharing your vision and plans for the future. You'll want to focus on the roles of your team and how they will personally contribute to this transformation. Your finale should sum up all the parts of your presentation, essentially following this pattern. Peel back the Wrapping (what your organization is), open up the Box (what your organization was), and reveal the Gift (what your organization will be).

Chapter 1 closes with a section about the importance of inspiring passion and keeping your vision fresh. I provided a series of questions you can ask to ensure you are constantly revitalizing your vision and encouraged you to revisit them regularly. This will keep your teams constantly anticipating the future and working with a daily sense of passion.

CHAPTER 2: The Gifts You Receive

In chapter 2, we delved into an equally important element of leadership: the gifts you receive. These gifts are the talents and contributions provided by members of your organization. To be a truly effective leader, you'll need to learn how to receive these gifts in a way that helps team members expand their skills and grow.

Anticipation plays an essential part in this as well, which I showed through my story of my friend Dr. Robert Welch and the four hats. This sense of anticipation functions as what I call the "passion pill," a catalyst that can help expand the capacity of your teams to achieve more ambitious goals. By understanding the role of anticipation in team dynamics, we can increase engagement, productivity, and the overall well-being of our employees.

Next I covered the importance of a leader's responses to contributions, or the way you should receive a gift. To illustrate this concept, I shared another personal story about Dawn and me, this time about her cooking skills early in our marriage. Despite the imperfection of her early meals, my positive response encouraged her to keep going, and today she's an excellent cook. Our organizations are no different—your reactions to the contributions of team members will define their future performance. To help you receive gifts effectively, I recommended three key practices:

- Clearly communicate your vision, ensuring everyone understands the big picture.
- Remain open to new ideas and show your passion for each person's contributions.
- Recognize the milestones your organization has reached and celebrate the individual achievements of your staff.

Chapter 2 closes by touching on the importance of vulnerability and the Gift Exchange Cycle. By receiving gifts properly, you can ensure that this cycle operates in a healthy manner. Part of this reception is remaining vulnerable with organization members by staying honest and using tools like active listening. By doing so, you can prevent the Gift Exchange Cycle from becoming dysfunctional (meaning contributions are ignored, undervalued, or poorly received). A dysfunctional cycle can demotivate your team and erode trust, leading to lower productivity and employee retention.

CHAPTER 3: The Atmosphere You Create

In chapter 3, we looked at how the atmosphere and environment of your workplace can define your organization's success. Scientific research backs up this claim, notably the study that shows the right environment can increase drive, commitment, and overall productivity.

Your employees should feel excited to come to work and confident that their workspaces will feel like their own. To accomplish this, you'll need to understand your teams on a deeper level by engaging in meaningful dialogues and learning about their characteristics and aspirations. Once you have this knowledge, you can start to plan the physical changes that your workplace will undergo.

From here, we looked at what it takes to create the ideal atmosphere and environment. I shared a few principles I follow when changing the physical attributes of a workspace, including:

- Functional Design: areas within your workplace that have distinct purposes and the necessary equipment to serve those purposes
- Metamorphic Spaces: areas that evolve and change with your organization
- Health and Safety: a health environment that complies with all safety regulations

- **Regular Feedback and Collaboration:** open feedback channels and inclusion of team members in the decision-making process

Chapter 3 closes with a section detailing the primary pillars that many successful organizational environments are built on. I call these the Three Cs: Core Values, Culture, and Community.

Core Values

The values that guide your company's decisions and actions. They should be physically represented in your workspace.

Culture

The way your core values manifest in the actions and decisions of your organization, including in the way you design specific areas.

Community

The way your core values and culture shape your interactions. The nature of these interactions will also inform the way you design your work environment.

CHAPTER 4: Roadblocks

In chapter 4 we dove into the roadblocks to leadership and the root causes behind common challenges. While these roots may seem small at first and may even contain beneficial elements, each has the potential to grow from a small, annoying weed into a tangle of serious issues.

I identified seven distinct roots that I believe many roadblocks stem from: tradition, communication breakdown, leadership tunnel vision, long-tenured employees, fear of investing, pride, and a lack of accountability.

- Tradition: Tradition can be a powerful force and may help an organization succeed in some ways but can also cause an organization to get stuck in a comfort zone.
- Communication breakdown: A disintegration of communication can be at the root of numerous issues and may lead to a culture of silence, in which ideas are withheld instead of shared.
- Leadership tunnel vision: Leaders who remain too focused on the future may miss important elements in the present, leading organizations to miss short-term objectives and let down employees.

- **Long-tenured employees:** Experienced employees can be incredibly valuable but may also be at the root of roadblocks. Complacency, resistance to change, and stymied growth can plague tenured team members, leading to a number of related issues.
- **Fear of investing:** Employers who fail to invest in their employees will find themselves with an unskilled workforce or low retention rates as team members search for greener pastures.
- **Pride:** Yes, it's important to take pride in your work. But too much pride could give leaders an overinflated sense of self-importance, and they may place themselves above their organization and team members.
- **Lack of accountability:** Leaders who don't take responsibility for their actions can undo even the strongest visions, leading to a cascading failure of accountability throughout their organization.

Chapter 4 closes with a few tips that leaders can use to navigate and overcome roadblocks:

- Embrace change and encourage innovation
- Foster open communication
- Balance vision with awareness
- Leverage long-tenured employees

- Cultivate a culture of accountability
- Address the fear of employee departure
- Regularly reassess and adjust strategies
- Celebrate successes and learn from failures

CHAPTER 5: Barriers to Leadership

In chapter 5, we tackled the barriers that stand between us and our potential as leaders. To overcome these barriers, you first must understand them. Many barriers are formed out of an inclination to seek comfort, which can unfortunately reduce our ability to grow. To fight this, we have to become self-aware and nurture our sense of empathy and emotional intelligence.

Strengthening these parts of our mind requires self-evaluation. I provided a set of questions to help you define your leadership style:

- What are my core values, and how do they influence my leadership style?

- What feedback have I received that I might have dismissed too quickly?
- How do my biases and assumptions affect my decision-making?
- How well do I understand the motivations and aspirations of my team members?
- What steps am I taking to foster a positive and inclusive work environment?
- In what ways have I demonstrated emotional intelligence in difficult situations?
- How do I react to failure, both my own and my team's?
- What am I doing to encourage continuous learning and growth in myself and others?

By answering these questions on a regular basis, you can assess how you are evolving as a leader and find any biases that are creating barriers. We all deal with biases, but to reach our potential, we need to identify and dismantle them. Then we will better be able to define our organization's goals and serve our team members.

Chapter 5 moves on to cover five common barriers I've seen in my career as a leader along with a potential solution for each:

- Team-selection bias
- Leadership-oriented environment creation
- Overemphasis on deadlines and schedules
- Self-centered perspective
- Micromanagement and delegation deficiency

This chapter closes with a section detailing the greatest barrier to leadership: a lackluster vision. Your vision needs to inspire passion, functioning as a living embodiment of what you and your team will achieve. If bureaucracy or bias cloud your vision, it likely won't succeed.

CHAPTER 6: The Bridge and the Apology

Our final chapter covered two essential components of leadership: the bridges we build within our organization and the apology, a tool that can help establish a clean slate for the future. It's essential that these apologies are not focused on you as the leader but on your team and your shared goals. This way, you show team members that you can take responsibility for your actions and make concrete changes moving forward.

Creating this apology requires a sincere desire to rectify past mistakes. You need to show humility and express a commitment to learning. You'll also want to establish a desire for open communication moving forward, shifting your organization from a top-down, results-focused structure to one that puts the team first. This doesn't mean results won't matter; in fact, you'll likely see an increase in not only profits and deliverables but also team satisfaction, retention rates, and the well-being of team members.

The chapter moves on to discuss how to establish bridges by having tough conversations. While these conversations may include criticism, it's important that they remain constructive. You'll also need to address your own faults first so that employees can see you aren't being hypocritical. Despite the challenge, these conversations can result in higher levels of trust, team cohesion, and overall morale.

After that, we discussed the sustainability of the bridges we build and how the value of your employees far exceeds their immediate output. The materials for these bridges are your core values, including principles like trust, integrity, respect, and an emphasis on teamwork. Goal-setting is essential here as well, as it can bridge the gap between where your organization is now and where it aspires to be. By reaffirming your goals and committing to the path ahead, you show that you're not only committed to acknowledging past shortcomings but actively working toward a better future.

BRING YOUR VISION TO FRUITION

Before we bring our exploration of leadership and organizational transformation to a close, I want to reiterate the essential components of my philosophy: anticipation and team-focused leadership.

Anticipation, the beating heart of our narrative, may be seen by the unenlightened as a mere feeling. But in the hands of a visionary leader, anticipation transforms into one of the most powerful tools imaginable. Anticipation is a spark, igniting passion, driving innovation, and aligning your organization to work toward a shared goal. As a leader, you have the task of nurturing this sense of anticipation, and you'll need three pivotal components: a clear vision, trust in your team, and a relentless focus on collective needs.

The clarity of your vision—the Gift, as we've referred to it throughout this book—is paramount. Merely *having* a vision isn't enough. You must articulate it so clearly and precisely that it becomes tangible and real for your team. This is an ancient concept that has existed throughout history, as we can see in passages like

Habakkuk 2:2: *Write the vision, and make it plain upon tables, that he may run that readeth it.*

This biblical wisdom underscores the necessity of a vision so clear and compelling that it propels your team forward, each member running with it, fueled by understanding and belief.

However, if you communicate your vision well, but the response from team members is still lackluster, you've reached a critical juncture. Such situations present two distinct possibilities: either you're not the right leader, or they're not the right follower. Removing this roadblock will require decisive action. A leader must recognize when to part ways with team members who can't muster a sense of anticipation or passion for the destination. Making these decisions is tough but necessary to ensure the vibrancy and forward momentum of your organization.

Ultimately, the hallmark of true leadership is selflessness. It's about stepping back and allowing the team to embrace and run with your vision. This allows you to build a culture where each team member feels trusted, valued, and motivated—not by someone else's dream but by the dream you all share. That's the foundational work of a leader: creating an environment where anticipation thrives, visions are clear and embraced, and the journey toward success is a collective endeavor.

Of course, the path to effective leadership is difficult to traverse alone. Elevated Leadership can guide you step-by-step in empowering your teams and making your vision into reality. I can personally share the strategies I've used in my many years of leadership experience to ensure that your organization is transformed into one defined by values, growth, and high employee morale. You can contact me at any time using the information below.

CONTACT INFORMATION
Michael Beard, founder and president of Elevated Leadership

Social Media
- Facebook: https://www.facebook.com/leadwithelevated
- Instagram: https://www.instagram.com/leadwithelevated/
- LinkedIn: https://www.linkedin.com/company/leadwithelevated/

Email: info@leadwithelevated.com
Phone: (352) 256-0424
Website: https://www.leadwithelevated.com/about

As we conclude, I want you to remember that perpetual growth and adaptation are a continual process. It is well known that Rome wasn't built in a day, but you have to remember, it also underwent many radical changes during each stage of its construction. Stay agile and humble while guiding others, always keeping your vision close at hand. Avoid rushing your vision's creation because it needs to be so compelling that it gives you chills. If your vision fails to resonate with your team, your transformational journey may be doomed from the start.

Embrace your role and demonstrate the dedication and passion you wish to instill in others. By doing so, you will witness the complete transformation of your organization, driven and unified by your vision. At the end of the day, your followers shouldn't just be saying "I'm ready to work." No, you want their eyes sparkling with anticipation and their voices echoing with excitement as they proclaim loudly, "I can't wait!"

ABOUT THE AUTHOR

As an accomplished speaker specializing in leadership, diversity, equity, and inclusion, Michael Beard has accumulated over twenty years of leadership expertise. Passionate about his work, he has helped numerous leaders in the for-profit, nonprofit, and educational spaces to enhance their productivity and surpass their achievement thresholds. Serving as the president and CEO of Elevated Leadership, he spearheads a platform that offers meaningful workshops designed to optimize work environments and cultivate trust within organizations. Michael firmly believes that a team is defined not merely by people working together, but by individuals who trust one another. Embracing this philosophy, he has empowered numerous leaders to enrich their organizations and realize their most ambitious objectives.

A proud alumnus of the University of Florida, Michael has spanned a diverse range of corporate and municipal environments in his career. He has been tapped for leadership training by prestigious organizations such as Bloomberg, Head Start Conferences nationwide, North Florida Center for Community Enrichment, My Village Project, and numerous universities across the United States. Additionally, Michael holds a certification from Cornell University as a diversity, equity, and inclusion trainer, further solidifying his expertise in these critical areas.

Beyond his professional accolades, Michael finds his greatest joy as a devoted husband to his lovely wife, Dawn, and as a father to their two sons, Deylynd and Terrell. His family life enriches his perspective, fueling his commitment to creating environments where trust and collaboration flourish.

www.ingramcontent.com/pod-product-compliance
Lightning Source LLC
Chambersburg PA
CBHW020241010526
44107CB00039B/1459/J